How to Become a Sport and Exercise Psychologist

Whether you are an athlete suffering from nerves or someone who lacks motivation to exercise, sport and exercise psychology can help. As the discipline of psychology evolves, more and more people are training to become sport and exercise psychologists. But how do you qualify, and when you do, what is the job really like?

This is the first guide to this fascinating and growing profession. It provides an overview of what the role involves, the educational qualifications and training you will need to take, and what those first few years in the job are actually like. It includes a wealth of tips on how to make the most of the opportunities available. The book also features testimonials from people currently working in the field, who reveal not only what helped them along the way, but also what they would have done differently.

How to Become a Sport and Exercise Psychologist is authored by two of the leading academics within sport and exercise psychology in the UK, both of whom have a wealth of experience in the field. The guide is the perfect companion for anyone considering this exciting career.

Martin Eubank is a Principal Lecturer in Sport Psychology at Liverpool John Moores University, UK.

David Tod is a Senior Lecturer in Sport Psychology at Liverpool John Moores University, UK.

How to Become a Practitioner Psychologist

Series editor: David Murphy, University of Oxford

David Murphy, FBPsS is Co-Director of the Oxford Institute of Clinical Psychology Training and a fellow of Harris Manchester College, University of Oxford. He is Past Chair of the Professional Practice Board of the British Psychological Society and has also been Director of the BPS Division of Clinical Psychology – Professional Standards Unit.

Psychology remains one of the most popular choices for an undergraduate degree, whilst an increasing number of postgraduate courses are directed either towards further academic study in a subdiscipline, or a career in applied practice. But despite the growing numbers of people interested in a career in psychology, from A-level students to those looking for a career change, the various pathways to entry into the profession are not necessarily obvious.

The *How to become a Practitioner Psychologist* series of books is aimed at providing a clear, accessible and reader-friendly guide to the routes available to becoming a practitioner psychologist. Providing both information and advice, including testimonials from those recently qualified, the series will include a title for each of the seven domains of psychology practice as regulated by the Health and Care Professions Council.

Each book in the series will provide an invaluable introduction to anyone considering a career in this fascinating profession.

How to Become a Counselling Psychologist
Elaine Kasket

How to Become a Sport and Exercise Psychologist
Martin Eubank and David Tod

How to Become a Sport and Exercise Psychologist

Martin Eubank and David Tod

Routledge
Taylor & Francis Group

LONDON AND NEW YORK

First published 2018
by Routledge
2 Park Square, Milton Park, Abingdon, Oxon OX14 4RN

and by Routledge
711 Third Avenue, New York, NY 10017

Routledge is an imprint of the Taylor & Francis Group, an informa business

© 2018 Martin Eubank and David Tod

The right of Martin Eubank and David Tod to be identified as authors
of this work has been asserted by them in accordance with sections 77
and 78 of the Copyright, Designs and Patents Act 1988.

British Library Cataloguing-in-Publication Data
A catalogue record for this book is available from the British Library

Library of Congress Cataloging-in-Publication Data
A catalog record for this book has been requested

ISBN: 978-1-138-93817-5 (hbk)
ISBN: 978-1-138-93818-2 (pbk)
ISBN: 978-1-315-67581-7 (ebk)

Typeset in Galliard
by Swales & Willis, Exeter, Devon, UK

Printed and bound by CPI Group (UK) Ltd, Croydon, CR0 4YY

Contents

Acknowledgements

The authors would like to express their gratitude to the Stage 2 qualification in sport and exercise psychology trainees who provided the testimonials contained in this book. Your voices give reassurance to those readers who are inspired to follow your lead and embark on the training journey you have had the courage and skill to take: thank you.

Introduction

David Murphy – Series Editor

Welcome!

First, I would like to welcome you to this book, which is one of a series of seven titles, each of which focuses on a different type of practitioner psychologist registered as a professional in the UK. One of the things that has always appealed to me about psychology is its incredible diversity; even within my own primary field of clinical psychology there is a huge range of client groups and ways of working. The books in this series are all written by practitioner psychologists who are not only experts in, but hugely enthusiastic about, each of their areas of practice. This series presents a fascinating insight into the nature of each domain and the range of activities and approaches within it, and also the fantastic variety there is across the different areas of practice. However, we have also made sure that we have answered the practical questions you may have such as "How long does it take to train?", "What do I need to do to get on a training course?" and "How secure will my income be at the end of it all?" We very much hope that this book will be interesting and answer all your questions (even ones you didn't know you had!) and further information and resources are available on our series website (www.routledge.com/cw/howtobecomeapractitionerpsychologist).

Psychology as a profession

Psychology is still a relatively young profession compared to many long-established professions such as law, medicine, accounting etc., however it has grown incredibly rapidly over the last few decades. One of the first people to use the title "Psychologist" in a professional context was Lightner Witmer who established what is widely recognized as the world's first psychology clinic in 1896 in Pennsylvania. Witmer came to study psychology after a degree in Economics and postgraduate studies in political science and then working for a time as a school teacher. He went on to study experimental psychology at the University of Pennsylvania and then at a famous laboratory in Germany. He went on to pioneer the application of experimental psychology ideas to the treatment of children with specific learning and speech difficulties.

At the beginning of the twentieth century, these early psychologists saw great possibilities in applying psychological concepts to help people achieve their potential. However, even they could scarcely imagine the scale and range of applications of psychology that would exist by the beginning of the twenty-first century. Psychologists now have well-established roles in schools, mental and physical health services, prisons, police and security services, multi-national companies, sport training centres; essentially almost anywhere where there is a focus on understanding and changing human behaviour, which is, of course, pretty much everywhere!

This book is, along with the other six titles in the series, intended to provide people who are at the beginning of their careers, or those who are thinking about making a change, with an insight into the different areas of professional psychology. We hope that you will not only gain an overview of what the specific domain of psychology entails, but also a sense of what it is like to work as a practitioner on a day-to-day basis. We also aim to explain how to become qualified to practise in the area of professional psychology, right from school until being fully qualified. Furthermore, we hope to provide an idea of how careers in the different areas of psychology can develop over time and how the profession of psychology might change as it continues to develop in the future.

Studying psychology at school or college

One thing that many people love about psychology is just how broad it is. As an academic discipline it encompasses the physiological workings of the brain and the nervous system, how we perceive sounds and language, how we make decisions and the treatment of mental health problems, to name just a few areas. In recent years psychology has become the second most popular degree subject at UK universities – indeed a total of 72,000 students were studying, either full-time or part-time, for a first degree in psychology in the academic year 2014–15.

Psychology has become not only a popular A-level choice but also increasingly an option at GCSE level. It is now possible, therefore, to take the first step on a career journey in psychology at an early age, and, if you are considering A-levels or GCSE subjects, we would certainly encourage you to look at psychology options if they are offered at your school. However, it is by no means required to have studied psychology at GCSE or A-level to follow a career in psychology. If you have already taken other subjects, or psychology isn't offered at your school, or you have decided to go for other subjects, this won't stop you going on to become a psychologist, if you decide that this is what you would like to do. Furthermore, contrary to some myths, psychology is considered a valid A-level choice for many other degrees apart from psychology; indeed it is listed as a "preferred subject" by University College London in their general list of A-level subject choices: http://www.ucl.ac.uk/ prospective-students/undergraduate/application/requirements/ preferred-a-level-subjects

The only GCSE subjects that are specifically required by UK universities to study psychology are maths and English. A-level psychology is usually listed as a "preferred" subject but is currently not required by any UK university for entry to a psychology course, and there is no indication that this will change. Therefore, overall our advice would be that psychology is an interesting subject choice which can provide a good foundation for further study in psychology, or other subjects. However, psychology at A-level is by no means essential for a career as a psychologist, so we recommend basing the decision on what your strengths and interests are and also what subjects are required for any other degree options you want to keep open to you.

Studying psychology at university

The first compulsory step on the road to a psychology career is attaining "Graduate Basis for Chartered Membership" of the British Psychological Society, commonly known as "GBC" (in the past this was called "Graduate Basis for Registration" or "GBR" for short). You will see this referred to a number of times in this book and the other titles in the series. The British Psychological Society (BPS) is the professional body and learned society for psychology in the United Kingdom. It was established in 1901 to promote both academic and applied psychology and currently has over 50,000 members, making it one of the largest psychological societies in the world. There are two possible routes to attaining Graduate Basis for Chartered Membership of the British Psychological Society on the basis of UK qualifications.

The most common route is to complete an undergraduate degree in psychology that is accredited by the BPS; a lower second class degree classification or above is required. This doesn't need to be a single honours degree in psychology; it can be a joint degree with another subject. However, in order to be accredited it has to cover a core curriculum that is specified by the BPS, and the provision must meet certain standards. At the time of writing there are over 950 BPS-accredited courses offered at over 125 different higher education institutions within the UK. Many of these courses are general psychology degrees; however, some focus more on specific domains such as forensic psychobiology, health psychology, abnormal psychology, sport psychology, business psychology, and so forth. Many are offered as psychology combined with another subject, and the array of possible options is extensive, including business, English literature, education, maths, history, philosophy, physics, zoology, and criminology, to name but a few. This range of choice could be a little bit overwhelming, but it is important to bear in mind that virtually all psychology degrees do offer a significant choice of options within them, so two students doing the same generic psychology degree at the same institution may actually take quite a different mix of courses, albeit still with the same core psychology components. Moreover, it is also important to remember that even if the title of a degree appears very specific, the course will still cover the same core psychology content.

For a career in professional psychology, the most important issue is attaining GBC. The subtle differences in the individual course content are far less important. Our advice would be to consider all the factors that are important to you about the choice of university and the psychology course rather than getting too focused on the specific content of a course. You may wish to do a degree that allows you to specialise in the area of psychology that you are particularly interested in, and of course that's fine. However, in reality, all postgraduate professional training courses need to cater for people with a range of different psychology backgrounds, so whilst having completed specialized options at undergraduate level might provide a good foundation to build on, it is very unlikely to mean that you can jump ahead of those who didn't do those options at undergraduate level.

My own experience was that I did a joint degree with psychology and zoology (I wasn't really sure what psychology was when I was choosing, so I hedged my bets!). Fairly early on I became interested in clinical psychology but I still got a great deal out of studying other subjects that weren't anything to do with clinical psychology, including many of the zoology subjects. In my final year, I did an option in vertebrate palaeontology (better known as the study of dinosaurs!), mainly because it sounded interesting. In fact, it turned out to be one of the most stimulating and useful courses I have ever studied, and the lecturer was one of the best teachers I have ever come across. I learned how to interpret inconclusive evidence by using careful observation and deduction rather than jumping to conclusions, and that generic skill has been very useful through my clinical psychology career. So my personal advice would be not to feel under any pressure to specialize in a particular branch of psychology too soon. I suggest you choose degree options because they are stimulating and well taught, *not* because you think they will look good on your CV. In reality, if you are applying for professional psychology training courses, what will stand out more on your CV will be really good grades which come from being really engaged and developing a thorough understanding of the areas you are studying.

Some psychology programmes offer a "professional placement year" within the degree. Such courses are often marketed on the basis that graduates have a higher employment rate on graduation. It is important to bear in mind, however, that you will also be graduating a year later than people on a three-year course, and during the placement year most people will be receiving little or no pay and still paying fees (albeit at a reduced rate) to the university. My own personal opinion is that degrees with professional placements don't necessarily offer an advantage overall. On the one hand, if a course does offer well-established placement opportunities, this can make it easier to get that first step on the ladder; however, there are many opportunities for getting postgraduate experience relevant to professional psychology, some of which are voluntary but many of which are paid.

The other main route to GBC is designed for people who have done first degrees in subjects other than psychology, and enables them to attain GBC by doing a conversion course. At the time of writing there were 67 BPS accredited conversion courses in the UK. Most of these lead to an MSc, although some lead to a Graduate Diploma; some are general in their content and are titled simply "Psychology" or "Applied psychology", whereas others are more focused on specific areas like child development, mental health or even fashion. However, if they are BPS accredited all of these courses will still cover the core psychology curriculum, regardless of their title.

Since the core components are common between all BPS-accredited degree programmes, you certainly will not be committing yourself irrevocably to any one area of professional psychology through your choice of psychology undergraduate or postgraduate conversion course. In the clinical psychology programme that I run, we take people who have a range of different experiences at undergraduate level, and some who did different degrees altogether. Of course, when you come to postgraduate qualifications, you do have to make more fundamental choices about the area of psychology you wish to focus on.

The different areas of psychology practice

The authors of each of the seven books in the series are, as you would expect, experts in, and enthusiastic about, their own area of psychology practice, and the rest of this book will focus pretty much exclusively on this specific area. Our aim across the series is to provide information about what each domain is about, what it is like to work in this area on a day-to-day basis, and what the route to becoming qualified is like. What we have not done, and indeed could not do, is say which one of the domains is "best" for you. The answer is that there is no one "best" type of psychologist. Instead, we hope you will be able to find the area of practice that seems to fit your own interests and strengths best. This can be difficult, and we would encourage you to keep an open mind for as long as you can; you might be surprised to find that an area you hadn't really thought much about seems to be a good fit.

Once you have identified an area of practice that seems to fit you best, we would certainly recommend that you try and meet people who work in that area and talk to them personally. Even after you have embarked on postgraduate training in a particular field, don't feel it is too late to explore other areas. Indeed, there are areas of overlap between the different domains, and psychologists with different training backgrounds might well end up working in a similar area. For instance clinical and counselling psychologists often work together in psychological therapy services in the NHS, whereas health psychologists and occupational psychologists might work alongside each other in implementing employee health programmes.

My own journey in professional psychology started with my degree in psychology and zoology, as mentioned earlier, and led on to postgraduate training in clinical psychology and then working in the National Health Service. However, my journey also included going on to be registered as a health psychologist and a clinical neuropsychologist, and I went on to do management training and became a senior manager in the NHS before moving into clinical psychology training and research in leadership development. Over the years, I have worked alongside colleagues from all of the domains at various times, particularly through roles with the British Psychological Society. I have been fascinated to learn even more about other domains through editing this series and, of course, as psychology is still such a young and dynamic field, new developments and new fields continue to emerge. I would, therefore, encourage you to think carefully about your career direction, but regardless of whether your psychology "career" lasts just for the duration of this book or the rest of your life, I would encourage you to maintain an open and curious mind. In the words of one of my favourite sayings, "It is better to travel well than to arrive." We hope this book, and the others in the series, will be of help to you, wherever your own unique career journey takes you!

What does a sport and exercise psychologist do?

Introduction

This chapter begins to map out the journey that will lead to you becoming a sport and exercise psychologist. You may be an A-level or undergraduate student studying psychology who's recently been introduced to the numerous specialisms that exist in the discipline and are thinking about career options. You may be a recent psychology graduate who wishes to pursue a career as a practitioner psychologist, or a doctoral researcher who would like guidance on how their academic career could lead to a professional role. You might also be someone from a non-psychology background who is considering a career change. Conversely, you may be lucky enough to have made the psychology specialism decision already, and undertaken an undergraduate sport psychology degree as the first step in your career plan. Whichever of these categories you're in, you are likely to be holding this book as someone who has an interest in a career as a sport and exercise psychologist. We hope that by the time you reach the end of the text you feel more clued up than you do at the moment. If so, then the read will have been well worth it!

Before you get further into the "nitty gritty" of this book and begin to learn more about the professional training journey to become a sport and exercise psychologist and what it's like, there will probably be two fundamental questions on your mind: What are sport and exercise psychologists, and what do they actually do? While we're sure you'll already have a preconception of the answer, and maybe even a pretty good idea, the aim of the chapter is to establish and extend your understanding by providing an overview of the job role and the requirements of it. With this in mind, we'll firstly consider what sport and exercise psychologists do, what types of people they work with, and what settings and environments they work in. Secondly, the chapter will get you to think about the important competencies, characteristics, and qualities required to be an effective sport and exercise psychologist. Finally, if you still like what you've read, the chapter will outline the professional training route you need to follow if you want to turn your interest in a career as a sport and exercise psychologist into reality. This will then be discussed in more detail in subsequent chapters, including the Master's and doctoral stages of training that need to be followed to open up possible career pathways within the domain.

To help you with this, we will draw on the testimonials of recent sport and exercise psychology trainees who describe, in their own words, what they do. The use of testimonials will be a recurring theme throughout the book, and we are confident you will find these "trainee voices" meaningful, impactful, and inspiring. Hopefully their stories will help you to feel less daunted by the prospect of embarking on the training journey involved, and will provide a different voice from ours that will further guide and reassure you. These are the very people who have been through the training route you are going to read about, and they represent success stories that you will look to emulate if you decide that a career in sport and exercise psychology is for you. To create the testimonials for the book, we asked the trainees to give us answers to the following questions. This chapter contains responses to section 1.

1: Overview of your job role as a sport and exercise psychologist

What do you do?

What types of people do you work with?

What settings do you work in?

What types of organizations are you employed by?

Are there opportunities for independent practice?

Options to work abroad?

What are the possible career pathways/progressions?

2: Work experience for the trainee sport and exercise psychologist

What do you need to think about in terms of gaining useful work experience?

What are the options available, and how do you make the most of your work experience?

3: Starting out

What issues might a new sport and exercise psychologist face when they first start the job, and how should you prepare for the experience?

What are the best things about starting out, and what are the challenges you'll need to overcome?

4: Applying for jobs as a sport and exercise psychologist

What should you think about when applying?

What are employers looking for, and how do you make your application stand out?

What will an interview involve, and how should you prepare for it?

Sport and exercise psychologists: what they do, who with, and where

Sport and exercise psychology is one of the newest of all the psychology specialisms, so it is a relative baby of the professional psychology family. That said, like most babies it has grown and continues to grow at a rapid rate. Sport and exercise psychology has been around in the UK as a discipline of sport science since the 1970s. The first sport science degree programme in the UK began at Liverpool John Moores University in 1975 and is still in operation today. It is testament to the way in which the discipline has established itself as a viable academic area of study with good job opportunities that students can now study degrees in sport and exercise psychology. It is only in the last decade that such programmes have begun to emerge, stimulated by the formal establishment of sport and exercise psychology as a recognized division of psychology within the BPS. Since the launch of the Division of Sport and Exercise Psychology (DSEP) in 2004, the number of full members has increased consistently over time, and at the time of writing it totals circa 820.

Sport scientists have been undertaking various forms of training to provide sport psychology support since the 1980s. It was as recently as 2008 – when the professional training route detailed in this book was created, followed in 2009 when the Health and Care Professions Council (HCPC) became the regulatory body for practitioner psychologists in the UK – that the opportunity to train to become a registered sport and exercise psychologist came into being. Since its launch, the BPS Qualification in Sport and Exercise Psychology (QSEP) has grown year on year, starting with around 10 trainees in 2009–10 to upward of 75 trainees in 2016. The number of trainees who have completed the programme since it began is approaching 30 (and counting!): this has contributed to the growth in the number of HCPC registered sport and exercise psychologists, which at the time of writing stands at 212 (87 female, 125 male). This is all good news for those interested in pursuing a career in the field.

As an example of the way in which sport psychology job opportunities have grown, consider 2016's Rio Olympics. If we were to review the number of sport psychologists who provided psychological support to UK Olympic athletes 40 years ago, we could probably count them on one hand, and the number may well have been zero. At the 2016 Rio Olympics, it would be unusual for an Olympic Sport UK athlete *not* to have a sport psychologist somewhere within their support system, and "on site" sport psychology support formed part of Team GB at the games. You will frequently have seen GB athletes recognizing the contribution of their support team in media interviews and online, with sport psychologists and other sport science specialists often being singled out.

Sport and its attitude to sport science have changed for the good over the last 40 years. There is now a much better understanding of the benefits that having a sport psychologist can bring, and the desire to tap into the discipline to find those "marginal gains" that might make the difference between gold and silver means that the job opportunities will continue to grow as long as there are people who want to be "faster, higher, stronger".

A trainee's voice

I combine my role as a lecturer in psychology with my applied sport and exercise psychology consultancy and work with individual athletes, teams, coaches, parents, and other important members of an athlete's support network. I have been surprised by the range of sports that I have been able to work in, which has included synchronized swimming, dressage, cricket, cycling, golf, tennis, wheelchair tennis, athletics, and football. I feel fortunate to be working as a sport and exercise psychologist at such an exciting time for our discipline and have witnessed a growing acceptance and support of sport psychology within academies and teams, and by sporting organizations. No two working weeks are the same, as clients train and compete all over the world. I can find myself immersed in a week-long training camp, pitch-side, in a classroom environment, or communicating with athletes remotely via Skype or telephone whilst they are away at events.

In outlining the nature and scope of sport and exercise psychology practice, the field is arguably the most diverse and broad of all the psychology specialisms. This is good for the career development and employability opportunities of those coming in, yet it makes the sport and exercise psychologist's role more difficult to define. This is a common concern of trainees who enter the domain and are trying to work out what, with whom, and where their work can be done. With this in mind, the BPS-accredited QSEP, which will be referred to in more detail throughout the book, provides relevant information to trainees on this question and has been used to inform this section (see www.bps.org.uk/careers-education-training/society-qualifications/sport-exercise-Psychology/sport-exercise-psycholog).

As a discipline in its own right, sport psychology attempts to understand the psychological factors that are affected by participation in sport. A sport psychologist may, for example, work to support clients whose motivation, psychological development, and emotional well-being is being negatively affected through their engagement in sport, whether this is at an elite, youth, or recreational level. At another level, much of what constitutes applied sport psychology is about how psychological factors affect performance. As such, a sport psychologist may assist clients – whether this be athletes, coaches, support staff, officials, or other relevant individuals – to enhance and optimize their performance. This is done through applied sport psychology approaches and interventions that help clients better understand or cope with their own experience of, for example, anxiety and self-confidence. Practitioners in sport psychology offer services to individuals and teams and the coaches, parents, or officials who have input into these athletes to target the athletes' performance enhancement and/or personal development. This helps athletes to prepare psychologically for the demands of competition and training, but also helps them to survive in and transition through sport throughout their career.

Sport and exercise psychologists typically focus in either sport psychology *or* exercise psychology. This is often down to personal choice and people's preference to work in one or other of those settings. There are those practitioners who successfully and legitimately work in both, but in our experience, the majority would typically describe themselves as sport psychologists and would use that title, with "pure" exercise psychologists being in the minority. There is certainly no better or worse practitioner here, just a diverse and broad domain where individuals often make a conscious choice about the role they wish to adopt. For exercise psychologists, a major focus is to seek to understand the life-enhancing and health benefits of exercise and how to promote lifelong participation. Exercise psychologists will typically work with individuals or organizations who wish to optimize the value of exercise as part of a healthy lifestyle. In this aspect of their work, exercise psychologists are primarily concerned with interventions targeted at the promotion of an active lifestyle which improve motivation and therefore increase participation rates in exercise and participants' adherence to it. There are also those clients for whom exercise represents a means of rehabilitation from illness, with direct referral of clients from health professionals such as dieticians and general practitioners or other community-based health initiatives. This will typically involve an exercise psychologist using behaviour-change counselling to create lifestyle adaptations in clients, and the provision of education and skills development services from allied health professionals, health trainers, and gym instructors to assist clients with their adaptation strategies.

A trainee's voice

Much of the work that I do toward having a performance impact for individuals is invisible to the player. This could be through educational presentations and workshops with parents and coaches or, as in the case of golf, training of caddies so they are better able to support the player. I would say that 50% of my applied work comes from individual athlete, coach or parent requests to develop mental skills and the other 50% from longer term contracts with sport organizations and governing bodies. Both can be very effective, although the latter enables a greater opportunity to build strong relationships and gain momentum with work. Rather than being solely reactive and working on client issues and challenges, you can start to be more proactive and develop psychological strengths.

Before we move on to talk about the competencies required by sport and exercise psychologists and the characteristics and qualities they need to be effective, it's worth stopping to think about the sport and exercise work settings described above and what they are actually like to work in. This is a key consideration for any aspiring practitioner, because having a real understanding of the sport and exercise environment is just as important as understanding yourself and the psychology you're delivering. It is common for practitioner psychologists to work in situ – e.g. in a training or competition setting where work is done in the real-world context. It is also important to recognize that sport psychology can be an interdisciplinary science, where the norm is to work closely with other sport sciences such as physiology, biomechanics, nutrition, and strength and conditioning to assist with athlete performance and development. The chance to work with athletes and other professionals at the site of their participation, training, and competition is one of the pleasures (and privileges) of being a sport and exercise psychologist. Being happy in your work is largely influenced by where you do it, so this means you have to understand the sport and exercise environment and be comfortable working in that world. But if you haven't worked in one of these environments before, how do you know what they are like?

It's true to say that not all sport environments are alike, and one of the most important tasks you will undertake in practice is to learn and understand the environment in which you and your clients operate. Many of these environments are extremely positive spaces in which to work, characterized by committed and dedicated people seeking to improve their performance and/or lifestyle within cohesive, structured, and supportive surroundings. When people are working together well and pulling in the same direction, the experience of being a sport and exercise psychologist in such settings can be hugely rewarding. Sometimes (typically at the elite sport level), there is a strong focus on performance (i.e. results), and outcomes (i.e. winning). This, and the fact the environment is full of competitive people whose jobs are reliant on results to get selected or retain funding, can impose pressure and an expectation to succeed that is quite a heavy burden to bear. The work of a sport and exercise psychologist is often focused on helping clients cope with the stressors that exist in high performance cultures, and the weight of expectation and responsibility on the sport and exercise psychologist can also be significant. The intention here is not to scare you off, but rather to paint a realistic picture of what working in sport can be like at times. Working at an elite level can be immensely satisfying, and you may be motivated and inspired by the sound of it. If you get the opportunity to work in elite/high performance sport, expect it to be an exciting but unique experience. Forming good relationships with influential people and searching for ways to make sure you are helping the client will be key.

A trainee's voice

In my current role, I have three different hats. I am employed by [college] as a senior lecturer in sport science and teach on a number of modules which have a sport and exercise psychology focus. I also lead the provision for the 200+ athletes based at [college] who participate in sports such as rugby, football, rowing, modern pentathlon, netball, golf, and equestrian sports. On top of this I run my own consultancy where I work with a number of athletes, teams, and also

(continued)

(continued)

business to try and help them reach their potential. Within this, there is great opportunity to work abroad and fully immerse myself within teams and groups of players. It's a busy life, but the variety of the work makes it so interesting: certainly, no day is like another.

The next section details competencies that will help you form good relations. Before we discuss these, it is briefly worth mentioning how service delivery often proceeds.

1: Intake

Beginning of relationship, establishing expectations and goals.

2: Needs analysis

Gathering information about your client's strengths, weaknesses, and ambitions/goals.

3: Case formulation

Synthesizing the needs analysis into a working model to guide subsequent decisions.

4: Choosing an intervention

Using your working model, scientific evidence, and professional judgement to decide the overall strategy.

5: Planning the intervention

Detailed planning of how your strategy will be structured and supported, and how it will progress towards its aims/goals.

6: Delivery and monitoring

The way the strategy and plan are monitored, evaluated and, where necessary, improved so that we know goals have been achieved.

Adapted from Keegan (2016).

The six stages described above represent a typical consulting process. Essentially, the key cornerstones of the sport and exercise psychologist's practice are the importance of getting to know your client really well and then formulating, justifying, planning, delivering, and evaluating your work with them.

If you decide to follow the training route outlined in this book, you will become very familiar with these features of consulting and will actively engage in them in your training. A trainee sport and exercise psychologist will learn to become effective in undertaking these steps with clients, but while they represent common fundamentals of doing applied work for all practitioners, there are many different ways to achieve them. Being able to do these well is important, but they are not the only things that will make you an effective practitioner. So let's have a look more broadly at the sort of competencies and qualities that are required and that you'll need to think about.

Competencies and qualities of the effective sport and exercise psychologist

To be an effective practitioner you need to become competent at what you do. In its application to practitioner psychology, *competence* is best described as our professional ability to engage in habitual and judicious evidence-based practice that is consistent with our education and training (Fletcher & Maher, 2014). To become qualified as a sport and exercise psychologist, competence is defined as attaining a threshold level that enables you to be fit to practise, such that you operate in accordance with specified and enforceable professional standards. Through their professional training, practitioners acquire *competencies*, which consist of the knowledge, skills, and abilities; behaviours and strategies; attitudes, beliefs, and values; dispositions and personal characteristics; self-perceptions and motivations that enable us to execute a professional activity like sport and exercise psychology effectively. It is also important to recognize that over the course of training and beyond, professional development never stops. It is a lifelong process. By definition, continued professional development (CPD) means that activity can be undertaken to help us learn and develop our practice expertise, and as a consequence create expert practitioners over time. The ongoing competence requirements for sustained effective sport psychology practice can then be derived from the practice of experts.

Sport and exercise psychologists are required to acquire competencies in the four key areas described below:

1: Competence in being able to develop, implement, and maintain personal and professional standards and ethical practice:

This involves compliance with the standards of conduct, performance, and ethics that should govern our work; a desire to develop and enhance ourselves as professional applied psychologists and incorporate best practice into what we do; a commitment to assure the integrity of ourselves and our discipline, the privileges and responsibilities of the profession, and the dignity, welfare, rights, and privacy of our service users by operating within our professional boundaries; and the ability to work effectively with other related professionals and adapt our practice to different organizational contexts of service delivery.

2: Competence in being able to apply sport and exercise psychology methods, concepts, models, theories, and knowledge in their consultancy:

This involves identifying service users' needs and assessing the feasibility of consultancy; determining the aims of consultancy and planning the objectives of interventions; establishing, developing, and maintaining working relationships with service users; conducting consultancy by implementing planned interventions; monitoring and reviewing the implementation of consultancy; and assessing and evaluating the impact of consultancy.

3: Competence in being able to conduct research that develops new sport and exercise psychology methods, concepts, models, theories, and instruments, and translate this and existing innovations to inform their practice:

This involves developing, designing, conducting, analyzing, and evaluating original sport and exercise psychology research to inform our applied practice, or to use research to solve a real-world problem that has been encountered.

4: Competence in being able to communicate and disseminate sport and exercise psychology knowledge, principles, methods to educate their service users:

This involves promoting sport and exercise psychology services and benefits to service users; feeding back information, and providing advice and guidance to meet an individual client's needs; and preparing and presenting information to individuals, groups, and organizations on the processes and outcomes of psychological interventions.

Adapted from British Psychological Society (2014a).

In summary, the competent sport and exercise psychologist is able to carry out effective consultancy- and education-based work that is research-informed and ethical in its practice. This should be complemented by attending relevant workshops, courses, and conferences that serve to enhance interpersonal consulting skills and develop a knowledge-base in working with a range of sport and exercise clients and service user issues. While it is beyond the scope of this chapter to talk about the range of different consulting philosophies, approaches, and techniques available to the practitioner psychologist, suffice it to say that there is a personal decision to be made here about *how* a sport and exercise psychologist actually chooses to work. This means that we don't all work in the same way, and there is a choice. Indeed, this choice is an exciting part of the training process, where you will discover the consultancy approaches you resonate with and those you don't. For example, might you use a more practitioner-led approach, such as psychological skills training, where the sport and exercise psychologist provides the expert lead in the client practitioner relationship and prescribes interventions as a means to enhance an athlete's performance? Conversely, might you resonate with, and be more congruent with, a more humanistic client-led approach, where the client takes more ownership and is empowered and facilitated by the practitioner, in a collaborative relationship, to find their own solutions? Alternatively, might you legitimately operate somewhere between the two ends of the scale? Finding the approaches that are a good fit for you is an interesting yet important part of the process. At the end of the day, probably the most important tool in service delivery competence is you, so spending time getting this right is definitely worthwhile!

A trainee's voice

I have two roles. The first is as a sport and fitness lecturer with the Open University and the second as a private consultant (sport psychologist). I predominantly work with elite athletes in individual sports (especially swimming and triathlon) through a university sport development centre and via the [governing body]. Although I get a number of requests for private consultancy, they tend to be from individuals rather than organizations.

As you might expect, sport and exercise psychologists are subject to evaluation from their clients, and this can often provide you with a useful and honest external assessment of how effective you are being. As practitioner psychologists we have a vested interest in knowing what makes us effective. Understanding the person behind the practitioner and the characteristics and personal qualities that make us effective at what we do is therefore a core consideration for the aspiring practitioner. When we ask coaches and athletes what they value in the service we provide, the themes listed below are common. As you read, you should think about these in relation to your own skill set and whether these are characteristics you feel you could develop. After all, these represent the things that you will need to "be" if you're going to succeed in this domain.

- Possess good interpersonal and communication skills.
- Be likeable and easy to relate to.
- Be flexible in your ability to address an individual athlete's needs.
- Be interested in and have a willingness to learn about the particular sport you're working in.
- Be willing to work with coaches to exchange thoughts and ideas.

- Be helpful, knowledgeable, understanding, and caring.
- Provide consultancy that focuses on an individual athlete's needs.
- Attend training sessions and competitions to gain an understanding of the sport and observe the service user.
- Be able to fit in and be honest, trustworthy, and professional.
- Be enthusiastic, positive, and constructive, and able to draw on an athlete's strengths.
- Be able to work as part of the team.
- Be a provider of a good practical service and provide concrete and practical solutions.

In addition to our clients, we can also learn from each other about what makes for effective sport psychology practice. From first-hand accounts of experienced sport psychologists, we know that effective practice results from being able to build trust and a working relationship, developing an effective programme, educating coaches, and increasing athlete confidence and cohesion in the consultancy process. This involves being able to identify the specific demands of the sport and adopt an individualized, athlete-centred approach. This is made possible by coaches and athletes being committed and receptive to what the sport psychologist has to offer, and by the sport psychologist being allowed sufficient one-to-one time with the service user. In contrast, ineffective practice tends to be caused by a lack of trust, not being adaptable, and failing to fit in with colleagues. This is corroborated by early career trainee sport psychologists' initial learning experiences of delivering psychological support. Trainees identified practice characterized by an ability to be flexible, comfortable with silence, and aware of the need for strong working alliances where the client and psychologist collaborated as being representative of effective practitioner development (McEwan & Tod, 2015).

In terms of what else works when working with athletes, we've also established that you need to know yourself, so self-knowledge represents a part of the journey that a trainee sport and exercise psychologist must willingly embark upon. Such self-awareness can be established by asking ourselves what needs we have, identifying our strengths and weaknesses, and understanding why we are striving to work in the sport psychology field and what we get from working with athletes. Increased awareness of self provides the practitioner with a deeper understanding of how we should "be" in the applied environment, and how our personal perspectives can influence the judgements and decisions we make in professional practice. At this point, it should be clear that what you know (your knowledge base) and how you do what you know (your practice skills) are necessary but not sufficient for effective practice. Interestingly, sport psychology literature tells us that those who have become excellent consultants *began* with certain personal qualities and experiences, suggesting that there are deeper aspects of a person that can form the basis of a successful consulting career. Put simply, the sport psychologist should be regarded as instruments in their own interventions, supporting the notion that a practitioner's personal qualities are implicated in their effectiveness.

Personal qualities represent aspects of the core self that relate to a person's morals, values, virtues, and beliefs. When sport and exercise psychologists have been asked about the personal qualities they need to be credible, trusted, and to survive in professional practice, authenticity, humility, openness, integrity, resilience, neutrality, and courage emerge as being fundamental (Chandler, Eubank, Nesti, & Cable, 2014), particularly when working in sport cultures, where dealing with conflict and failure is commonplace (Eubank, Nesti, & Cruickshank, 2014).

The text that follows contains quotes from research we have undertaken with sport and exercise psychologists (Chandler et al., 2016), which provide examples of what some of these qualities mean in the applied context.

Authenticity – engendering trust:

"I feel others trust me most of the time, and if you don't have authenticity I think you need to recognize that you've got to do something about it, and then you just go in there and be consistent in yourself, you don't change."

Authenticity – engendering genuineness:

"You've got to be genuine and have a very uniform approach to everything, not just switch it on and off: people will very quickly find you out if you're false."

Authenticity – engendering willingness:

"Be prepared to stick your head out a little bit and get it cut off, be prepared to upset a few people to get change. . .and stay true to what you want to do. If you go in and you're not really sure what you want to do, you'll get eaten alive."

Humility – engendering a desire to learn from others:

"I learn more from coaches, actually asking for their help and advice. . .that's probably something that psychologists don't do that much, as opposed to just being the person who comes in and solves the problems or resolves stuff."

Humility – engendering a desire to go unnoticed:

"I do a good job that I'm happy with, but not particularly to impress other people. . .not many people actually notice. . .I think that's really important. I'm not an expert in other people, what they think and what they know. They're an expert on themselves, I'm just helping them to know it."

Humility – engendering a desire to be behind the scenes:

"I make sure the people that matter recognize what I'm doing, but then if someone else wants to say it's their idea and they've done it then I let them get on with it."

Navigating the often uncertain, frequently unpredictable, and sometimes volatile terrain of sport and exercise can be difficult, particularly when you strive to work in a professional and ethical manner. What is clear is that having and being able to use these personal qualities will help you do that! We are strong advocates of exploring the deeper and more personal features of the practitioner and the person behind them, given it is this, in part, upon which practitioners can build a rigorous philosophy of practice and a trusting user–practitioner relationship. Self-exploration of who you are as a psychologist requires time and attention and is a personal and evolving activity. It involves meaningful dialogue about how personal qualities can help you to manage yourself in your work context and resolve the difficult challenges you will encounter in your practice territory.

Much of this self-discovery will occur in the process of professional training, but it could actually start now, as you read. Before making a decision to embark on the training required to become a sport and exercise psychologist (which we are about to describe in the final section of this chapter), you might ask yourself whether you recognize any of these personal qualities and characteristics in yourself, and if not whether you are willing to develop them to become an effective practitioner.

A trainee's voice

As an applied sport psychologist, I mostly work with athletes on a one-to-one basis. I have provided sport psychology support to athletes from a wide range of sports. These consultations can be in various settings, such as consultation rooms at the university, a cafe, the training environment, the athlete's home, or a quiet room in the athlete's training venue. Athletes might approach a sport psychologist for a wide range of reasons. For example, they might be returning from an injury, their performance may have dropped, or they may no longer be enjoying their sport. Sometimes the athlete's issue specifically relates to sport. For example, they might want to learn mental strategies to improve their performance, or they might not be getting on well with their coach. Other times, problems outside of sport, such as problems at school or university, are impacting their experience within sport. In addition to one-to-one work, I also deliver interventions to sports teams and run "taster workshops" that introduce sport psychology to groups of athletes. I have also helped coaches to introduce psychology into how they train athletes and prepare them for competition.

Outline of the professional training route to becoming an HCPC registered practitioner

The psychology profession is now regulated by the Health and Care Professions Council (HCPC), who hold a register of practitioner psychologists who have met their standards. Later chapters in the book will go into more specific detail about the key stages and features of sport and exercise psychology professional training. In outline, the route is characterized by a series of qualifications that commit the trainee to at least six years of work. This takes dedication, and you need to feel able to commit if you want to become a sport and exercise psychologist.

The first stage of training is to complete a BPS-accredited psychology undergraduate degree (normally three years full-time) at university, which if completed with a 2:2 degree classification or higher enables you to be eligible for Graduate Basis Chartered Membership of the BPS (commonly referred to as GBC). Many students will undertake a general psychology undergraduate degree before embarking on a specialized counselling, clinical, or sport and exercise psychology Master's qualification at the next stage. However, there are now a number of universities that run BPS accredited undergraduate sport and exercise psychology degrees, which also confer GBC but provide a more domain-specific educational experience while still containing the core psychology content required for the degree to be BPS-accredited. When we see prospective students on open days at our own university, we stress to them the importance of doing an accredited degree that confers GBC. We're giving you the same clear message here! Not all degree courses in psychology are BPS-accredited, and they may have a genuine reason for not being so: e.g. if it's a joint course but doesn't contain an adequate amount of psychology. For someone aspiring to be a practitioner psychologist, it does come as a bit of a shock when we tell them they can't become a sport and exercise psychologist without GBC, which they could have obtained by doing an accredited undergraduate programme in the first place! That said, if, for whatever reason, you have undertaken a psychology first degree that was not BPS-accredited, it is possible to undertake a GBC conversion course before the final stage of training (normally before or after the Master's degree) which provides the knowledge in core areas of psychology not attained through the first degree. It isn't uncommon for students interested in science and sport to undertake a sport and exercise science degree on gaining entry to university either. While these programmes aren't normally BPS-accredited, as they don't include sufficient psychology content within their validated programme structure, there are many students who genuinely don't know on entry to such a course that sport and exercise psychology might be their career path.

As a tip, if you undertake a sport and exercise science degree and realize six to 12 months later that you want to be a psychologist, it may be possible for you to transfer to an accredited psychology degree programme via direct entry into year 2 if the GBC material hasn't been taught in year 1. It's worth asking the question, as it may save you a year of time having to do a GBC conversion course! That said, there are also many people who come into professional psychology after taking a non-psychology first degree and later doing a psychology conversion, so don't be put off if you have started off on an unrelated subject: what matters is where you end up, not where you start from, and people from diverse backgrounds contribute greatly to the profession.

The second stage of training is to complete a BPS-accredited Stage 1 Master's degree (normally 1 year full-time or 2 years part-time) in sport and exercise psychology. There are a number of these courses across the UK (see the next chapter for a list) that provide the "knowledge bridge" between the undergraduate degree and the final "practice" stage of training. Stage 1 is essentially about the mastery of a sport and exercise psychology knowledge dimension, the content of which is specified by the established BPS accreditation criteria to which these programmes must align.

More specific detail about the Master's stage of training and what should be learnt from the programme content can be found in the next chapter. At this point, though, we would extend the same "health warning" about accredited and non-accredited Master's provision that we issued earlier, in relation to undergraduate programmes. There are some Master's programmes that contain sport and exercise psychology material but are not BPS-accredited. This is not a reflection on the quality of the programme or the learning experience provided, but for someone who is committed to becoming a sport and exercise psychologist and following the training route, these programmes aren't, in that regard, helpful. Again, be careful and ask the BPS-accreditation question! In the same way that the GBC conversion course provides the means to get you back on the professional training route, there is a mechanism do to the same at master's level if you get diverted, but it does cost money and time. Universities with BPS-accredited Master's programmes in sport and exercise psychology will have academic regulations governing what they commonly refer to as recognition of prior learning (RPL) or accreditation of prior learning (APL). Through this mechanism they can award academic credits for certain aspects of certified learning that match their own programme provision. This means that someone who has acquired academic credits in sport and exercise psychology from a non-accredited Master's could be granted RPL for these credits by another university.

It's true to say that different universities have different rules about how much RPL credit they can give. In the best case scenario this would probably enable 120 of the 180 M-level credits to be awarded, but you would have to enrol on the accredited Master's at the "new" institution to complete the remainder, which is likely to involve another research project. While we see this as no bad thing for your CV, it does mean more study (and more money and time) to acquire the Stage 1 award you need. If you want our advice on how to make it easy on yourself, it would be to do an accredited programme to ensure that four years after you started, you end up where you should be!

Once you've reached the final stage of training (Stage 2), you will begin the process of developing the competencies you read about earlier in this chapter. Stage 2 is referred to as the practice dimension, which is where, as a trainee sport and exercise psychologist, the applied work required to become a fully qualified practitioner psychologist is done over a minimum of two years. The HCPC approve Stage 2 programmes that align to these standards and produce sport and exercise psychologists who are eligible for the HCPC register, of which QSEP (referred to earlier in this Chapter) is one. HCPC registration is essential to practice. Note that it is illegal in the UK to use the term "practitioner psychologist" or "sport and exercise psychologist" or any derivative thereof in advertising services to the public unless you are on the HCPC register. Without following the current professional training route we have articulated, it is not possible to credibly or lawfully practise as a sport and exercise psychologist in the UK.

Stage 2 training is based on the principle of supervised practice, where a trainee's work is quality assured and supported by a registered sport and exercise psychologist who is also an experienced and qualified supervisor of trainees. There are two ways to complete Stage 2 training and become HCPC registered. Firstly, you may choose to enrol on the BPS Stage 2 QSEP, which provides trainees with an independent route to acquire the ethical, consultancy, research, and communication competencies required. Through a process of planning your training, then conducting your work and submitting examples of your research, case work, education, and dissemination activity and consultancy/ethical reflections for assessment, you hope to emerge as an HCPC registrant (as well as being a BPS Chartered Psychologist). Then your career as a sport and exercise psychologist really begins! The other option you may wish to take is to complete a Stage 2 professional doctorate at a university. While structures may differ from course to course, these are required to meet the same Stage 2 accreditation criteria and standards and are in effect equivalent in that regard to QSEP. You should therefore expect to engage in planning, conducting, and reflecting on sport and exercise psychology through the production of research and consultancy work. Given that Stage 2 follows Master's Stage 1, which follows undergraduate degree study, "Prof. Docs" are what we refer to as doctoral (D) level study. While D level is a requirement of Stage 2, only universities have the capacity to confer academic awards, so the completion of a professional doctorate carries with it the doctor title typically given for a PhD. Their appeal, therefore, is that successful completion of a professional doctorate in sport and exercise psychology entitles you to a doctoral award from the relevant university, chartered psychologist status from the BPS if the course is accredited by them as the professional body, and HCPC registration subject to course approval. This is quite an attractive "all inclusive" package!

There are numerous pros and cons to each of these two training options. The independent route qualification (QSEP) works well for those who want complete independence and flexibility in their training and supervision and cannot – or do not want to – commit to a university-run programme that is more structured. For some trainees, the independent route can be a little isolating, but working in group supervision settings and organizing peer-group networks is a good way to alleviate that. Aside from the obvious pro of the professional doctorate being able to confer a doctoral award, some trainees like the more structured approach afforded by a university programme, where access and proximity to supervisors, fellow students, potential placement providers, academic staff expertise, and learning resources is guaranteed.

The decision to enrol in a university professional doctorate or the BPS independent route is certainly a significant one. If you embark on a professional doctorate in sport and exercise psychology, check with the programme provider that it has the necessary BPS accreditation and HCPC approval pending or in place. Beyond that, the HCPC and BPS standards that the training programmes are aiming to develop are the same.

Summary

On reaching this point, we anticipate that you'll have a better understanding about what a sport and exercise psychologist does and how to become one than when you started reading the chapter. What should be apparent is that the role is multifaceted and can engage you with a diverse range of clients across a "participation to high performance" continuum and place you in a range of operational settings. It is in these roles, across this continuum, and within these environments that you need to be effective. We also hope the chapter has given you some clear idea as to how effective sport and exercise psychology is gauged, and the skill sets you will need if you still have the ambition to become a sport and exercise psychologist. The chapter describes a number of key competencies that need to be developed if you are to consult and educate in a research informed and ethical manner. What we also hope you've realized is that one of the most important tools in applied practice is you. As a practitioner, your own personal qualities form a significant part of what makes you an effective sport and exercise psychologist, and we have encouraged you to begin to consider "the person behind the practitioner" before embarking on the journey towards becoming an HCPC registered sport and exercise psychologist.

The professional training route you need to follow in order to reach this destination is outlined at the end of the chapter, but you now need a more detailed explanation as to how each stage contributes to becoming a sport and exercise psychologist. The next two chapters in the book look in more detail at the territory of these stages of training, with a specific focus on the standards and content of accredited sport and exercise psychology Stage 1 Master's programmes, followed by the post-Master's Stage 2 qualification options for becoming a trainee sport and exercise psychologist. As with the previous chapter, in the next two chapters we will again draw on the testimonials given by our sport and exercise psychology trainees in discussing their experiences of becoming and being a trainee. This includes some useful insights into how they gained and made the most of work experiences along the way which emerged in response to the questions below:

Work experience for the trainee sport and exercise psychologist

- What do you need to think about in terms of gaining useful work experience?

- What are the options available, and how do you make the most of your work experience?

3 | Psychology graduate – the next step

Introduction

You may already know, or be able to contemplate knowing, what it feels like to reach the end of three (or more) years' hard work to graduate with your BPS-accredited undergraduate degree. This is always a proud achievement, but for the aspiring practitioner psychologist it represents the first qualification on the professional training journey. While the undergraduate degree puts you at the door to a career in psychology, the decision about which domain of psychology to choose isn't always obvious. Some graduates will open the door with a firm grip, purposefully striding through to confidently locate the sport and exercise psychology domain. Others will hold the door more gently, slowly opening it to peep through at what lies on the other side, and then tentatively stepping through to gaze at the counselling, clinical, occupational, health, sport, and exercise and other options on offer, and then ponder their next step.

In our years of experience teaching on a sport psychology Master's programme, we recognize these two different experiences in the faces looking back at us in the classroom on day one. The point we're trying to make here is that while it's great to be sure that sport and exercise psychology is your destiny, it's also OK and normal to be a bit unsure. Our advice to you is to take your time, speak to as many knowledgeable people as possible about the different domains of psychology and what they represent in career terms, and read books like this. These are the things that will help you to make your decision, which is, after all, a very important one. We say this because, unlike your accredited undergraduate degree, which offers you the opportunity to step into any domain of psychology you like, the domain in which you choose to do your Master's degree will dictate your professional training direction and career trajectory. For example, completing a BPS-accredited Stage 1 Master's degree in sport and exercise psychology is an entry requirement for Stage 2 sport and exercise psychology training programmes. While, of course, people can and do retrain to change career direction, it is preferable, from both a personal and a financial perspective, to make an informed decision now, at this point, about where the sport and exercise psychology profession road can lead. In our experience of graduates in this position, the main reasons for uncertainty centre on their perceptions about employability, their enjoyment of more than one domain, or confusion about domain "crossover".

We often find ourselves having detailed discussions with prospective students to clarify the sport and exercise psychologist's role (discussed in Chapter 1) and the numerous employment opportunities that exist in the public, private, and self-employed sectors. If you're prepared to consider the incredibly diverse range of service users – from junior to senior, recreational to elite, individual to team, participation to performance (we could go on) – the sport- and exercise-engaged (and disengaged) population is vast. Is there crossover between exercise and health psychology? Yes. Do sport psychologists encounter organizational or clinical issues? Often. Can sport and exercise psychologists use counselling psychology theory and skills in their approach to practice? Definitely. That said, the issue here is that like all practitioner psychologists, sport and exercise psychologists are "bound and boundaried" to work in the sport and exercise psychology context and with the competencies that a sport and exercise psychologist is trained to possess. This means that their work should be done in settings where sport and exercise psychology expertise is being used and applied within the boundaries of competence defined by our training (not beyond them). There may be instances where a sport and exercise psychologist might need to refer someone on to, or recruit the services of, another type of practitioner psychologist; for example, when an athlete has clinical depression and anxiety and requires the expertise of a clinical psychologist.

Psychologists from other domains will be able to have similar conversations with you and define their roles and boundaries: while this is beyond the scope of this book, it is certainly something for those unsure of their psychology domain of choice to get clear information about.

A trainee's voice

While there are lots of factors to consider, perhaps one of the most important is how any work experience fits with where you'd eventually like to be. In short, will it start to build the skills that you need to achieve your ultimate professional goals? For example, if elite sport is your target, then seeing how other support disciplines work (and how they interact with sport and exercise psychologists) can help to build an early interdisciplinary picture. While often easier said than done, finding a coach who buys into sport psychology can also be vital – this can really make or break what you can and can't do and try out. Also consider working in sports or settings that you're not familiar with to emphasise "the psychology" of what you're doing. Indeed, if you know the sport or setting well, then apparent development and effectiveness might come more from other factors (e.g. credibility, tactical knowledge, talking the language). This is of course not "wrong", but it might mask the need to develop other, perhaps more fundamental skills that are otherwise not exposed.

Now that's out of the way, we will assume, given you've taken the trouble to buy or borrow this book, that a career in sport and exercise psychology is at least a possibility for you. On that basis, the book will now explore what you should expect to learn from a BPS-accredited Master's degree in sport and exercise psychology, and the important contribution it makes to your professional development.

Approaching a Stage 1 Master's degree in sport and exercise psychology

A BPS-accredited Stage 1 Master's degree in sport and exercise psychology is regarded as the "gold standard" through which the underpinning knowledge relevant to the practice of the sport and exercise psychologist is acquired. As such, these degrees are recognized by the Health and Care Professions Council (HCPC), in that the Stage 2 training programmes the council approves rely on entrants having completed a related BPS-accredited Master's programme. If you want to get onto the HCPC register, you need to do one of them.

At the time of writing there were 19 of these courses in the UK, and it is up to you to decide which one you wish to study. More information on relevant BPS-accredited Master's programmes can be accessed via the BPS website (www.bps.org.uk).

While all these courses carry the important BPS accreditation and therefore meet the same educational standards and core content to a benchmark level of quality, their "healthy" differences lie in the way in which the programmes have been designed and structured to meet these standards. In other words, each programme will have its own distinctive philosophy about what it is intending to achieve and how it is doing it, and an ability to understand how this translates into a quality student learning experience. In our experience, the depth to which particular sport and exercise psychology concepts (more detail about what these are is provided later in the chapter) are covered in an accredited programme is a good reflection of the research expertise and applied experience of the academic staff delivering them, and can give the programme a distinctive identity. These factors, coupled with the profile and reputation of the staffing base itself and the standing of the school/department and university in which the programme resides represent key points of distinction. It's a good thing, in our view, that our accredited courses are not identical: instead they contain some academic freedom for the course provider in choosing how to meet the required standards, and this gives you the opportunity to shop around and select the product you like the best.

From your perspective, the only given is that the programme you are contemplating is accredited against the same academic criteria, so unless your motivation to study at a particular institution is its geographical proximity to where you live or where you would like to be, then, as with other service industries, you are able to shop around. While you can browse online and get basic information from programme websites and fact-files, we would suggest that the best way to get a true feel for a product is to go and "browse in store". This is the best test of whether a particular course is a good fit for you. . .and you for it. What looks good on paper can often prove to be ill-fitting when you try it on for size, and may come nowhere near your expectations of what you hoped it would be. Most universities will run postgraduate open days/events at which staff will be present to discuss their courses with you. We suggest that you grab this opportunity with both hands and engage them in the dialogue that will truly tell you how good the course is. Firstly, when you speak with them, establish whether they are enthusiastic and passionate about their programme, sport psychology in general, and even being part of the open day. If they appear disinterested or a little ambivalent, or it seems that they would rather be at their desk writing their latest research paper, that isn't a good sign! Secondly, ask about the programme philosophy and for more detail about its module context and structure. If the programme provision is high quality and well-planned, you should expect an assured and comprehensive answer to this question. Most programmes will be advertised on universities' websites, which allows you to do your basic research first and then ask specific questions when you visit. Expect to get the answers you're looking for: you shouldn't be fobbed off by being told to look at the website you've already read! Finally, if you ask about the career and employability opportunities in the field, you should receive a positive response that gives you a sense of optimism that there will be opportunities to work in the sport and exercise psychology domain and the motivation to undertake a postgraduate course. Course providers should also be familiar with the BPS professional training route and what options are required to become a registered sport and exercise psychologist. We attend many postgraduate course events like this, where we get to talk to people who've visited many places when contemplating this important decision. Our comments are based on our insights from prospective applicants, so don't assume: go and find out for yourself and do everything you can to ensure you're happy with your choice.

A trainee's voice

Getting some hands-on experience is really useful before even starting your training as a psychologist. I think one of the most important characteristics of a successful sport psychologist is to develop the skill to simply become part of the sporting team. Although psychology experience can be quite hard to come by, helping out with teams and supporting athletes in the simplest ways can give you access to high performance environments. From there, making the most of placement modules on university courses to give you the most hands-on

(continued)

(continued)

experience as a psychologist will also give you a head start when it comes to working with athletes on your own as a psychologist. Get experience of working with others to build strong relationships, so any experiences you've had being student mentors, youth support workers, counselling would be useful. I think it's important to show that you are good, or have had experience at developing effective relationships with others. Also develop an attention to detail and a creative mind. Showing that you can problem-solve or come up with interesting ideas would again help you stand out from the crowd.

Once you've carefully selected your course, you need to apply for it. Remember that this is the university's opportunity to scrutinize you as thoroughly as we've suggested you scrutinize them. While the aim is to provide about as many places on courses as there is demand, some courses are in high demand, and so securing a place may be a competitive process. Hence you really need to pay attention to what will make your application stand out. All courses have an undergraduate entry requirement (normally a first or a 2:1), but that's simply a given to get you past the "reject" filter of the course admissions administrator. As people who look at many Master's applications on an annual basis, our tips on this are two-fold: Firstly, make sure you select two referees who know you well and are likely to write you thorough, well-informed, and timely references that reflect your academic ability and skills in psychology/sport and exercise psychology and the personal characteristics and motivations that make you suitable for the programme. It is both considerate and in your best interests to give them enough time to write the reference. There's nothing worse than asking politely for a reference, then in the next sentence apologizing for the fact that you need it in 24 hours! The probability is you won't get it. Secondly, put every ounce of effort you have into your personal statement. Assuming that your qualifications and references are OK (which they often are), this is probably *the* piece of information in your application that will determine whether you receive that precious offer or not. The personal statement should be about you, your motivation/passion for psychology/sport psychology, your personal experiences and involvement in sport and exercise, your related career experiences and ambitions, why you want to do a Master's, and why *this* Master's. Do your homework on the course you're applying for: if you demonstrate that you've read up on the course and its aims, structure, design, content, and staff and why that fits with you, it shows you've "gone the extra mile" and probably share the same vision and passion for the course as the person writing the course's marketing material. In fact, it's highly likely that whoever's written this marketing material will be the person who reads your application! We can assure you that investment of this nature will be time well spent and just might make the difference in securing that all-important offer. Last, but by no means least, do a grammar and spelling check and proofread your application. We hope we're preaching to the converted, but you'd be amazed at what we see. In a competitive selection process, don't make it easy for the recruiter to reject you, which they will if your application is full of sloppy phrasing and typos.

Once you've secured your offer, you should consider approaching your Master's study with the same motivation, diligence, and passion that you put into the application that got you there. Good Master's students share these fundamental characteristics, and they devote time and energy to their attendance, their engagement in taught classes and tutorial sessions, and their independent reading and research activity. This professional attitude to study resonates well with what is, after all, a professional training route to a professional career.

Students often ask what they can do outside their Master's course to help their career. Often the real question being asked here is "Can I do applied work and/or can I shadow someone else doing it?" While this enthusiasm is great to see, our answer is often tempered with information that is more about what you can't do at this stage than what you can, and a reminder that post Master's you still have a minimum of two years' training to do under supervision before working as an independent practitioner. While this can be frustrating for some, it is important for our domain's professional standards that Master's students understand where the boundaries are and where the "line in the sand" must be drawn. So, avoid applied work involving any form of consultancy and intervention where you are providing psychological support to elicit some form of behaviour change. Whether it is the athlete who wants you to help them develop their concentration, the team who want you to make them more cohesive, or the coach who wants to develop a more mentally tough mind set, all of these real-world examples will likely involve some form of intervention. You are not at the stage in your training where this activity can legitimately take place: nor are you ready! You can observe someone else do this form of work, but that is not always easy to engineer given the client–practitioner relationship and the confidentiality agreements they have in place, so don't expect it. Our advice is to gain relevant experience that may not involve directly shadowing a sport and exercise psychologist. For example, gaining experience of developing working relationships with people, or spending time in sport and exercise environments to observe and learn more about their organizational culture are extremely valuable activities for graduates and will help you to develop relevant core skills and knowledge. We would also advise Master's students to think about other CPD opportunities they could engage with to develop their knowledge and understanding outside of their chosen programme. For example, becoming a student member of their professional body – i.e. BPS – and engaging with the activities they provide is a useful way to develop. This may involve attending divisional workshops, training events and conferences, or doing short courses that will broaden your learning. In this network you will also be able to talk to both registered and trainee sport and exercise psychologists about their work, which is a great way to get different perspectives on applied practice.

A trainee's voice

Be prepared to be flexible, and to accept that the people who have agreed or asked you to help them might have very different ideas about what they want from you than what you would like to be doing or think would make most sense in that placement. We all leave our Master's degrees with lots of big ideas about how to help athletes, and lots of those ideas are great, have an evidence-base, and work in practice. However, sometimes all you are being asked to do is a handful of generic sport psychology workshops. You may well get frustrated that you can't do as much as you would like. If you try to do more than you are being asked or being paid to do, you could damage that relationship, and/or you could burn out. Just try to do whatever you are being asked to do as well as you can, learn from the experience and reflect upon it. In terms of looking for the right training experiences – sometimes you need to be pragmatic and opportunistic and take something because it's there. Other times, you might be in a position to create training opportunities for yourself (e.g. by offering to do some work with a particular athlete or team or gym) where you are able to be more in control of what you do.

The core and specialist taught components of a Stage 1 Master's degree in sport and exercise psychology

Once you arrive to start your BPS-accredited Master's in sport and exercise psychology, what should you expect to study and learn? Each programme must teach and assess you on particular core and specialist taught components that represent the underpinning knowledge and critical understanding required by the sport and exercise psychologist. An easy-to-understand guide is outlined below, but more detailed information on the relevant BPS standards for Master's programmes in sport and exercise psychology can be accessed visa the BPS website (www.bps.org.uk).

Research and research methods:

Learning about the research methods used in sport and exercise psychology and how to conduct your own sport and exercise psychology research

Sport and exercise psychology in practice:

Learning about the ethics, approaches, and core skills used by the sport and exercise psychologist in their applied practice.

Cognitive processes:

Learning about cognitive processes in sport and exercise psychology – e.g. the effect of competitive anxiety on anticipation and decision-making in sport.

Psychological skills and strategies:

Learning about the psychological skills and strategies used by the sport and exercise psychologist in their applied practice – e.g. the use of an imagery intervention to enhance an athlete's self-confidence, or the use of counselling approaches to develop psychological well-being.

Developmental processes:

Learning about developmental processes in sport and exercise psychology – e.g. the career transition experiences of athletes.

Social processes:

Learning about social processes in sport and exercise psychology – e.g. the coach–athlete relationship, or group dynamics and team cohesion.

Participation and well-being:

Learning about participation and well-being issues in sport and exercise psychology – e.g. the psychology of eating disorders, burnout, and injury in sport, or exercise adherence and addiction.

Individual differences:

Learning about individual differences in sport and exercise psychology – e.g. motivation, mental toughness/resilience, confidence, personality, and self-concept/esteem.

Reproduced from British Psychological Society (2014b).

Acquiring this knowledge and understanding will also help you to develop core skills central to sport and exercise psychology practice, such as the ability to *think critically* about the current theory, methods, and practice you learn about, to *use, apply, communicate, and disseminate* a range of relevant techniques and methods integral to professional practice, and to *self-reflect* on your developing professional identity as a trainee sport and exercise psychologist as you go! This skill development will be really useful if you want to progress to Stage 2 training, which will be discussed in more detail in the next chapter.

Now you know what a Stage 1 Master's degree in sport and exercise psychology is all about, think again about the importance of looking at all the different courses on offer and how they have chosen to deliver the taught components and associated skills outlined above. In their flexibility, programme providers will have developed a curriculum that meets these standards of education and training while making the most of their particular strengths in research and practice to give the programme a distinctive identity and philosophy. One other issue to consider in this regard is the balance of sport psychology versus exercise psychology in the programme. There are many psychological concepts and skills in this domain that can be researched and applied through both a sport and an exercise lens. For example, we might be interested in how an elite athlete maintains their motivation to train, or how a sedentary individual establishes a motivation to adopt exercise. You can expect the sport and exercise lenses used to help you understand these concepts and skills to differ from programme to programme. If a programme carries the title MSc Sport and Exercise Psychology, it means that at least 25% of what you are taught comes from the sport area and 25% from the exercise area. Hence the programme could be 75% sport plus 25% exercise psychology or the other way around, or even 50/50. Programmes that have less than 25% of an area will be titled sport psychology or exercise psychology. Of the programmes currently available, approximately 85% carry a sport and exercise psychology title with the remaining 15% being titled sport psychology.

Why might this be important to you? Well, you might want to study a programme that has at least a quarter of its taught content devoted to both sport and exercise psychology. If this is the case, another question to ask the programme provider is how much of their course is devoted to each area. Alternatively, you might want to study a programme that places more of an emphasis on sport, which might reflect the setting you want to work in as a registered practitioner. For example, if you feel that you want to work as a registered practitioner psychologist in sport (not in exercise), then a Master's programme that places more emphasis on sport might be for you. Again, you need to talk to the programme providers about how much, if any, exercise psychology content is in their programme, just so you know what to expect and whether it fits with what you want.

A trainee's voice

When I began training as a sport psychologist, I enjoyed meeting new people and offering these people something that they found valuable. During my undergraduate degree and Master's degree, I spent a lot of time reading, writing, and conducting research. I didn't actually spend much time with athletes or coaches until I began my supervised training. I enjoyed meeting athletes and coaches during my supervised training and trying to offer them something valuable, based on what I had learned during my studies. It was also interesting to learn how the research and theories that I had read about in text books and journal articles actually applied in "real life." Sport psychology issues are typically "messier" in real life compared to academic texts, and so learning to apply research and theory is an interesting challenge.

Summary

The decision to choose and then undertake a Stage 1 Master's degree in sport and exercise psychology is an important one that will play a large part in determining your future career direction. It was our intention in the first part of this chapter to share experiences as academic recruiters, and to reassure you about the questions to ask when you are making your choices about which domain and then accredited course to study. We've argued that you should go into this process with your eyes wide open to all the facts (plus the myths and misconceptions), get a sense for what each course and experience might be like, and go for the one that gives you the best fit and feel. Sport and exercise psychology is an increasingly popular career choice, so places on accredited Master's programmes are becoming increasingly more competitive to secure. To be offered a place on the course you really want to study, we can't emphasize enough the importance of a high-quality application, where a thoughtful, well-constructed personal statement will really make you stand out and will go a long way to getting you your place. We've given you our perspective on what we look for in a good personal statement, so we hope you find that useful in preparing your own.

Towards the end of the chapter we gave you information about what an accredited sport and exercise psychology Master's programme will look like in terms of its core and specialist content and the knowledge, skills, and understanding you'll need to acquire. Ask the right questions to help you decide on the right course for you (we've given you some clear pointers about this), and do think carefully about the issue of the proportion of sport versus exercise we discussed at the end of the chapter. This will be returned to in the next chapter, where the context of the choice you make to train in sport *and/or* exercise settings will be considered.

Now we're moving on: Once you graduate from your Master's – and it would be nice if you did so with a merit (60%+ grade average) or even better a distinction (70%+ grade average) – you have reached Stage 2 and the final key step in becoming a sport and exercise psychologist. The next chapter discusses that part of the journey in some detail, and what is involved in becoming and being a trainee.

4 Becoming a trainee

Introduction

To recap, the professional training route to becoming a sport and exercise psychologist involves the completion of a BPS-accredited undergraduate degree, followed by an accredited Stage 1 Master's in sport and exercise psychology and finally a BPS-accredited and HCPC-approved Stage 2 qualification in the domain of sport and exercise. At this point in the book, the undergraduate and Stage 1 Master's components of the training route have been discussed at some length, so it is now time to focus on the final Stage 2 element of the training process. It is in this period of training where, informed by the knowledge acquired from the preceding undergraduate and postgraduate programmes, the applied practice competencies integral to becoming a sport and exercise psychologist are developed.

"I'm a trainee sport and exercise psychologist." When you utter these words to your first client – a much-anticipated yet daunting moment for most trainees – you will have just enrolled on either the BPS Stage 2 QSEP or a professional doctorate in sport and exercise psychology to complete your professional training. The Stage 2 QSEP was launched in 2008 as the only route to the HCPC register for aspiring sport and exercise psychologists in training at the time. It focuses on the development of a plan of training that enables competence in ethical and research informed consultancy and dissemination to be developed through work with clients in "real" sport and exercise psychology settings under the supervision of an HCPC-registered sport and exercise psychologist.

In recent years, some of the universities offering Stage 1 Master's programmes have extended their taught provision to develop BPS-accredited and HCPC-approved professional doctorates in sport and exercise psychology. These programmes are delivered by the university and are based on the same Stage 2 standards as the BPS QSEP. Hence they are equivalent programmes. HCPC registration is a product of both, so you only have to study one of them to be eligible to apply to the HCPC's register. The difference between the two is largely based on two issues: The first is that unlike the BPS, a university is able to make academic awards to those who successfully complete a programme of study. As Stage 2 training in sport and exercise psychology is completed to doctoral level, the opportunity to acquire a doctorate from a "Prof. Doc" is seen as an additional benefit. Secondly, while QSEP and professional doctorates both involve supervision of work-based/placement learning in sport and exercise settings and rely heavily on a good working relationship between trainee and supervisor, QSEP is otherwise an independent route, where trainees take full responsibility for their professional learning. While a professional doctorate also expects trainees to have the ability to work independently, their professional learning is supported by taught sessions and associated material developed specifically to help the trainees' professional development. In short, the university-based professional doctorate engenders a more structured learning experience. As alluded to in a previous chapter, there are pros and cons to each training approach. Your choice can be made on the preferred nature of the learning experience for you as a trainee, without having to worry about one modality being better or worse than the other.

A trainee's voice

After finishing a master's degree in sport psychology, the road to becoming a psychologist is still long (likely two to three years). I completed the first 18 months of my supervised training while working a full-time job, and I completed the second 18 months while studying for a PhD. This meant that I needed to complete a

(continued)

(continued)

lot of my studying and gain experience working with clients in my evenings, weekends, and time off work. This can be tiring. I highly recommend meeting with other trainees regularly. Meeting with others helps you to realize that you are not alone in your experiences and that others are facing the same challenges as you are facing. Meeting with other trainees also gives you the opportunity to share your learning experiences and to learn from theirs.

After four years of acquiring lots of knowledge and skills from your accredited undergraduate and Master's degrees, you now get to do applied work with real clients and gain direct experience of the realities of professional work in the sport and/or exercise psychology domain! This chapter discusses the key steps you need to take to become a trainee, and the key features of this final stage that you need to success-fully navigate in order to become fully qualified. Being qualified to work independently and without supervision (as a consequence of completing your professional training and applying to become HCPC registered) and starting out on that part of the journey is the focus of Chapter 5, but before you reach that point there's still a significant amount of important professional training and development that must be under-taken. When you emerge from the training cocoon, you need to be ready to stand on your own two feet as an autonomous practitioner. So what, in training terms, gets you to be ready for that moment?

A trainee's voice

The biggest issue as a trainee (or as a newly qualified sport and exercise psychologist) is the feeling of incompetence. Developing and nurturing a peer network of other trainees (or other SPs) is really important in combatting this – very quickly I realized I was not alone and others felt the same. As a trainee I found that by engaging with others and discussing our experiences in time we all realized that we actually weren't doing too badly. I would recommend that very early on in an individual's training he/she should read around the narratives of neophyte practitioners as there is a wealth of advice out there in respect of how to manage these normal fears.

Levels of competence

As a reminder from Chapter 2, the Stage 2 training process aims to give you the opportunity to develop competence in four key areas. These are phrased as self-statements you should feel confident about making at the end of your training:

1. I feel competent in being able to develop, implement, and maintain personal and professional standards and ethical practice.

2. I feel competent in being able to apply sport and exercise psychology methods, concepts, models, theories, and knowledge in my consultancy.

3. I feel competent in being able to conduct research that develops new sport and exercise psychology methods, concepts, models, theories, and instruments, and translate this and existing innovations to inform my practice.

4. I feel competent in being able to communicate and disseminate sport and exercise psychology knowledge, principles, and methods to educate my clients.

It is also important to remember that the level of competence required in these four areas of Stage 2 training is designed to be congruent with doctoral qualifications. This means that the Stage 2 experience, be it QSEP or a professional doctorate, must enable you to do applied practice and research that is *rigorous, independent, original, informed,* and *critical* in your conceptualization and evaluation of it. In short, this is advanced stuff, but you can take comfort in the fact that the training you'll already have done to this point will have prepared you for it, and that will continue throughout your Stage 2 experience. To help with this, you will need a good plan and a good supervisor. Hence there are a number of important decisions in becoming a trainee that centre on supervised practice. In deconstructing this topic, there are two obvious key considerations for you: 1) what will your practice in training actually look like, and 2) who will supervise it?

A trainee's voice

Early in my training, I found it useful to approach as many people as possible about gaining experience. I contacted club coaches from

(continued)

(continued)

every sport I could think of in my region, and I provided information on the service I could offer them. I also contacted people who could help me to contact lots of athletes who might be interested in sport psychology support. For example, a university sports union was willing to forward my introductory email to all people who were registered with this sports union. Lots of student-athletes then contacted me to say they would be interested in working with a sport psychologist.

The nature of sport and exercise psychology training practice

In planning your training, you first need to decide how long to enrol on Stage 2 for. Can you do it in two years as a full-time trainee, or do you need to go for a longer part-time equivalent? The answer to this question will depend on your individual circumstances and the time you have available to devote to training. To give you an idea, 460 days of sport and/or exercise psychology-related activity is required on QSEP, so this is a significant undertaking. If you're working part-time and your job isn't sport and exercise psychology industry-related, it's probably more realistic to take additional time to successfully complete this stage of training. If you're already in a related job or are continuing as a full-time student, then two years is more feasible. The actual cost of the qualification itself isn't likely to be affected too much, if at all, by this decision, so you could enrol for longer to spread the cost if that helps.

You also need to consider and then detail how you will develop the required competencies. You need to do around 160 days of actual applied work with clients in addition to your research, CPD, and independent study, so you need access to applied settings in which to work. Apart from those (few) individuals who are employed by one sport organization full-time, most sport and exercise psychologists work across a range of settings, especially if they're self-employed. This is no different in training. It's likely you will undertake a number of work-based learning activities, commonly referred to as placements. These will be with a variety of different clients, potentially wide-ranging in their duration, and take place across a range of different environments. Examples include requests to develop and deliver a series of education sessions across a variety of different populations and periods of consultancy work with a diverse range of individuals or teams using the consultancy process outlined in Chapter 2. Unlike other domains of psychology, it's unlikely you'll undertake all your applied work-based learning in one place – for example, with one team, individual or organization where your engagement is frequent over a long-term period. Given the varied nature of sport and exercise psychology consultancy, it would actually be disadvantageous to do this, as it would risk you becoming narrow in your exposure to different sports and clients. When it comes to getting a job or securing clients as a freelance practitioner, having only experience of working with, for example, male footballers, or frustrated golfers, or inactive kids isn't going to make you as attractive to potential clients as those practitioners who have much broader experience. If you want a career in this field you'll need it to be able to pay the bills, and then pay for the lifestyle you want, so put yourself in a position to be able to work across a range of clients and settings if you want to earn well. You might land the "big fish" contract one day, but that's not guaranteed, and it's best not to spend your entire career trying at the expense of everything else!

A trainee's voice

Early on in the training process I think that there needs to be a willingness to work for nothing. Very few athletes will be prepared to pay for services of someone with little experience. Eighteen months into my training I was afforded the opportunity to work with an elite swimmer (gratis); however, that individual started recommending me to other swimmers and to the coach and this opened up my first paid work. Many of my early opportunities came from my supervisor, [and] this is an important aspect of selecting a supervisor. It is worth asking whether they will have opportunities for work for candidates.

When considering what sort of applied work to do in training, the sport versus exercise psychology question becomes relevant again. You may decide to plan work that is entirely sport- or exercise psychology-based, or to combine the two in whatever ratio you want. Coincidentally, although the HCPC protected title is "Sport and Exercise Psychologist", this includes any derivative of it. Many practitioners prefer to call themselves a registered sport psychologist, for example, if that better reflects what they do.

To help you think about what might be classed as relevant applied training experience with clients in both these contexts, it is useful to know a bit more about what "relevant experience" might be. Relevant applied consultancy in sport psychology can be gained from working with male and female athletes, coaches, parents, and support staff at club, regional, national, and international level across team and individual sports, for example. While this represents the sort of client diversity we advocated earlier, be aware that access to some populations, especially high-level athletes, is a limited resource, particularly during training. Don't be surprised if you find that difficult. There's no rule that says you have to work at that level, and in most cases you aren't ready anyway. In our view, it's probably best to "learn your trade" with athletes from local, district, or county teams. This will probably be a more worthwhile and rewarding experience anyway, and certainly less stressful! While it's natural to want to select the sports in which you have an interest, we'd also advocate taking yourself out of this comfort zone and doing work in other settings that you know less about in order to build up your experience and skill set.

A trainee's voice

Throughout my training, I found it really helpful working with clients who were as varied as possible. I worked with athletes, coaches, and teams from a wide range of individual and team sports, male and female athletes, and athletes who were 13–70 years old. This gave me experience working with a wide range of sport issues and adapting my service to different populations of athletes. If you have the opportunity to observe or shadow other sport psychologists, perhaps in a team environment, then make the most of this opportunity by asking lots of questions. Be willing to ask them how they made particular decisions. What influenced what they decided to do? If you observe training or a match with them, ask them to share their thought processes with you. What are they thinking as they watch the athletes perform?

Relevant applied consultancy in exercise psychology may be gained from primary and secondary care referral schemes, where clients require psychological support for disease/illness rehabilitation. Community-based health programmes involving lifestyle adaptations and behaviour change intervention are also common settings for exercise psychology work, often in liaison with health trusts and trainers. Commercial settings (including private and public gyms) and corporate wellness programmes are becoming more prominent opportunities to offer psychological support in assisting behaviour change and lifestyle adaptations. Many groups also provide training for their staff in behaviour change and the psychological facets of client work, so you may be able to get involved in assisting in the education and skill development of allied health professionals, health trainers, and instructors.

Becoming a trainee sport and exercise psychologist does not come with a salary attached. The client groups identified above are probably constrained to "sport and exercise psychology on a budget" or even looking for support on no budget. Although as a trainee you don't expect to command the fees of a fully qualified professional, it is hard to do all your applied work on a voluntary unpaid basis. Nonetheless this may be the reality, and it may therefore be wise to expect nothing, so that anything you do get is a bonus. You might, for example, be able to negotiate coverage of your expenses. If you aren't fortunate enough to secure a paid role with a team, don't let that put you off. At this stage acquiring the hours is the priority, and similar experience could be gained by offering free sport psychology support to a team or a squad of individuals. As you build up your contact hours and begin to demonstrate value to the client over time, this may attract a financial return, although there is no guarantee. That said, we know students who have started their own business during Stage 2 training and have become financially independent – it is entirely possible and increasingly common. Just remember that it will all be worth it in the end!

A trainee's voice

I had a background in professional golf and although this would have been the most tangible route to work I felt that it was important when

(continued)

(continued)

training to work in other sports. I found that if I was speaking to a golfer I made too many assumptions about their particular performance issues. I was too quick to think I knew what they meant by, for example, low confidence, as I would confuse this with my own experience. If a synchronized swimmer suggested they had low confidence, I would have to get a full picture of that experience from speaking with them and observation of them in training and competition. Whilst immersing yourself in the sport is vital in order to be effective, your interest and expertise is in human behaviour and performance and so you do not need to have experienced the sport previously. Build a network across a range of sports with key individuals, e.g. coaches and heads of sport science, detailing clearly what you are looking to do. I found that the most useful experiences came from providing presentations and writing magazine articles on sport psychology topics, often free of charge. This exposed me to wider audiences and individual consultancy opportunities always came from this initial investment of time.

Understanding the "supervised" in supervised practice

Who will supervise your practice, and what does supervision entail? In the context of this stage of professional training, whether it be on QSEP or a professional doctorate, practice under supervision is an integral part of a trainee sport and exercise psychologist's preparation for independent practice. As such, supervision is defined as:

> a personal interaction between the Sport and Exercise Psychologist in training and their supervisor for the purpose of addressing the trainee's needs and performance. . . it may take place by means of face-to-face meeting, telephone conversations and/or email communications. Supervision may also occur between supervisors and groups of trainees.
>
> British Psychological Society (2014a, p. 10).

Stage 2 sport and exercise psychology training is an experiential process designed to gain direct experience of the realities of professional working in relevant contexts and develop practical skills and the ability to integrate theory and research into practice. The intended outcome is to turn you into a competent psychologist who is eligible for HCPC registration. As such, your professional development should be supported and guided by an experienced professional – a role filled by a good supervisor.

So what should you expect from a supervisor? Well, the first thing you should know is that they are trained, either by the QSEP-approved supervisor training programme or their university in the case of a professional doctorate. Some supervisors will be eligible to supervise on both types of programme. Not all HCPC-registered sport and exercise psychologists are qualified to supervise, so it is *you* who decides who your supervisor is going to be (even on a professional doctorate there is likely to be more than one potential supervisor to choose from). You need to "go shopping" again (in the same way we suggested for choosing a Master's course) to find out who's out there and what's on offer. This is another key decision in your career development, so take your time. Remember that as defined above, this is a "personal interaction": you will spend two years or more being supervised by this person or team, so it is vitally important that you like them and strike up a good working relationship that will make your training experience meaningful and enjoyable. Also, the training process can be arduous and stressful at times, and it is important that you feel your supervisor is someone you can turn to in times of need when, inevitably, you need to share your anxieties and offload your frustrations. Like all good psychologists, they should practise what they preach, and be there to listen, show empathy, and regard, and above all care about your well-being as a trainee.

While supervisors will differ in their style of supervision, they will be relatively consistent in what they do, as the expectations of supervisors in this regard are part of the training they receive to do the role. You should be able to regard the list below as typical for all approved supervisors, but it's still worth exploring how the person you've identified as a potential supervisor will undertake the activities included on the list.

    i. Carry out a needs analysis at the outset of your training;
   ii. Oversee the preparation and review of your Plan of Training;

iii. Conduct regular meetings with you during each year of your training using face-to-face, Skype, telephone, and email communication methods as appropriate, and agree/be flexible on the frequency of these;

iv. Provide you with academic, ethical, organizational and professional information relevant to your training;

v. Provide you with guidance on work-based learning opportunities necessary to complete your applied practice hours;

vi. Observe, or arrange for you to be observed, working in a practitioner situation;

vii. Encourage you to reflect on your learning and practice and to engage in creativity, problem-solving and the integration of theory into practice;

viii. Listen to your views and concerns regarding your work in progress and offer appropriate advice;

ix. Advise and guide you on the production of your work for assessment.

British Psychological Society (2015, p. 11).

What else is important? Well, pragmatically, you might want to ask your supervisor what sort of clients they've worked with and what existing contacts they have available to help you build up your client base and applied practice hours. While they are all competent supervisors, someone who has a good applied network and experience of working in the sorts of environment and setting you're most interested in might be more appealing. Also, while all supervisors can perform their role across sport and exercise settings, not all will have the same experience in both, so you might feel that matching your requirements to their experience in this regard is something you'd find useful.

It is also appropriate to ask about their experience as a supervisor. How many people have they supervised? How many are they currently supervising? (You might even be able to talk to some of them.) Do they have space/time for you? The definition of supervision given above referred to the potential for it to be done across "groups of trainees". While there should be time for one-to-one supervision, there are distinct advantages in being part of a training group. Firstly, it gives you the opportunity to discuss your work with other trainees (and vice versa), which allows you to share good practice, problem-solve, and learn from each other. Such environments are really productive. Secondly, it gives you the opportunity to share your personal and professional development experiences in a safe space with others who are going through exactly the same things as you are. Trainee sport and exercise psychologists often have very positive experiences, and that is something to celebrate with others, to give you positive reinforcement and confidence. That said, there will be occasions where practise won't go as you wanted it to. In the welcoming and empathetic "arms" of the training group, you can find comfort and empathy and eventually an ability to celebrate the fact that when things go wrong this generates powerful learning experiences that make you a better practitioner. In our experience, without this sort of network sport and exercise psychology training can be quite an isolated experience which some cope with better than others, so from that perspective we think it's a perfectly valid and reasonable question to ask a potential supervisor.

More philosophically, we'd also be inclined to ask the supervisor how they practise and how they view your development in this regard. We commented briefly in Chapter 2 on the importance of having a clear philosophy of practice that is congruent with your own core beliefs and values about human nature, function, and change. This is something that you are striving to develop over the course of your training, but your supervisor should already know what theirs is and should be able to give you a definitive answer! We feel it is important to know the practice philosophy underpinning the person/people training you, and whether that sounds like something you could ascribe to. That said, good supervisors won't attempt to create trainee clones of themselves: instead, they give time and attention in supervision for you to explore who you are as a psychologist. They recognize that this is a personal and evolving activity, but even so, it is plausible that their philosophy will influence yours. A degree of congruence, or at least not complete dissonance, between the two of you is probably something to establish before you commit.

Finally, back to pragmatics again! Unlike a Stage 2 professional doctorate, where supervision cost is built into the course fee, the price of supervision on the independent QSEP route is down to what different supervisors decide to charge. In the same way that you would shop around for the best phone contract, discuss price openly with each supervisor you sound out. It is certainly worth doing some research in the area before committing yourself as prices do vary. The price is not an indicator of quality: rather what the supervisor feels is value for money based on what they are giving you. Having done your research, which contract you decide you take out is then up to you.

Summary

Having reached this point in the book, you will have gathered information about all the various stages of the UK sport and exercise psychology professional training route, and some of the key considerations and content/structure elements that support the provision. Once you successfully reach the end of the training route, you are deemed to have acquired knowledge and developed competencies that enable you to practise independently and without supervision. This means you are eligible to apply to the HCPC to become a member of their register and legally use the title "Sport and Exercise Psychologist". At this point, the "trainee" tag can be dropped, and you are free to fly the nest and embrace your new-found autonomy. In this chapter you have also learnt about some of the important *ongoing* considerations for the trainee during their professional development, including the importance of effective supervision. We, and many of the trainees who have completed the process, believe that there is great benefit in seeking to continue the supervisory relationship and membership of your trainee network *post-registration*. Don't become isolated: there is strength in numbers, and a problem shared (confidentially of course!) is a problem halved. Maintaining contact with a supportive network and having an experienced peer mentor throughout your career is never a bad thing. Most supervisors are only too willing to be a "supervisor-cum-mentor" for life. We encourage all trainees to embrace this notion.

The next chapter explores one of the biggest steps you will take in your early professional career, and explores the experience of starting out as a sport and exercise psychologist. The chapter draws on previous work we have undertaken to offer some insights into the features of starting out that you will likely encounter and need to learn from.

To add further perspective about this important career transition, we have provided trainee testimonials that identify the issues and challenges a new sport and exercise psychologist might face when they first start the job, and how they can best prepare for the experience. The trainee voices you will read are formed from their responses to the questions below:

Starting out

What issues might a new sport and exercise psychologist face when they first start the job, and how should you prepare for the experience?

What are the best things about starting out, and what are the challenges you'll need to overcome?

5 | Starting out

Introduction

The time when you emerge from your Stage 2 training "cocoon" as a fully qualified sport and exercise psychologist will be a defining but critical moment in your career. During these types of critical moments you are transitioning from being a student to being a qualified autonomous practitioner, and you will probably feel both anxious and excited as you come to grips with your new identity (Nesti & Littlewood, 2011). You no longer need to operate according to the requirements dictated to you by your lecturers, teachers, and supervisors, but will be free to assist clients in the ways you see fit (but still within the ethical boundaries provided by the HCPC and BPS!). Although you will have increased confidence and a sense of freedom to choose your own professional destiny, you may also have some doubts about whether you can "make it work" and earn a living. It may help to learn that these feelings are normal, and if you did not feel like this then we would wonder how motivated you were to pursue your goal of helping athletes. One recent Stage 2 graduate said: "Once qualified, these concerns reappear, the competent confident trainee [I was] becomes a newbie again." Her self-doubts arose from realizing that she had less access to the "safety nets" previously provided by her teachers, mentors, and supervisors from Stage 1 and Stage 2 training. She was now accountable for her choices, behaviours, and mistakes.

The initial months and years that pass after you embark on your career are intense and engaging and are a time of considerable change, as you apply your knowledge and skills for financial, personal, and professional reward. In this chapter we will present some of the challenges and issues that individuals typically experience when starting out, along with the sources of assistance and knowledge that help them cope, survive, and thrive as sport and exercise psychologists in the UK.

The trainee's voice

I was consistently told prior to commencing my training that there is not enough work to be a sport and exercise psychologist, but I have never found this to be the case. Whilst it is true that there may be less full-time, permanent positions than colleagues who work for example in clinical or forensic settings, there is not a sport that I have been involved in that does not recognize the importance of sport and exercise psychology support. If you want the stability of a regular working week then perhaps working as a sport psychologist does not currently offer that. If, however, you are passionate about sport at all levels, like to travel and work as part of a team and if you feel you have the discipline and dedication that is required to run your own business, then everyone involved in sport and exercise would benefit from training and development in this area. That suggests to me that it may be more accurate to say there are not enough psychologists to meet the growing demand!

Challenges

Effectiveness

One of the initial desires newly qualified practitioners experience is to see themselves and their interventions helping clients. They are interested in applying their knowledge and skills to athletes and exercisers to show they can help people and make a living. They have positive feelings when they receive encouraging client feedback, especially as they discover ways to apply their skills to new athletes, sports, and exercise contexts. With time, practitioners begin to realize that creativity is a feature of the job, because although clients may have similar issues – such as anxiety, motivation, difficult coach relationships, and desires for love, approval, and respect etc. – the ways they are expressed and the situations in which these matters play out are almost endless.

There are few "textbook clients". Early in sport and exercise psychologists' careers, before they have begun to observe parallels among clients and the same issues repeating themselves, almost every athlete or exerciser provides an intense learning experience. One new sport and exercise psychologist, for example, said "every hour that you spend with a client is actually a useful hour" (Tod, Andersen, & Marchant, 2011, p. 105). At the same time, newly qualified practitioners start to find out the boundaries and limits of what they can do. Most client issues are just what they appear to be: relatively straightforward and typically focused on sporting performance or exercise achievement. But sometimes, practitioners come across clients whom they are unable to help. One of co-author David Tod's first clients was a gymnast with an eating disorder. Not being trained as a clinical psychologist, he could not provide help and had to refer the client to a suitable practitioner. It was a valuable learning experience, and David started to learn as much as he could about eating disorders so that if another client with the same issue came along he could understand the individual and say the right things to encourage the person to seek help. It was still a surprise, however, for David to come across an issue that was different from those he had read about in the textbooks and discussed in class.

Practitioners also learn that sometimes the typical sport and exercise psychology mental skills training interventions discussed in the scientific literature (e.g. goal-setting, imagery, relaxation, and self-talk) are not suitable for the issues that clients raise when first meeting them. Typically, when sport and exercise psychology textbooks describe the interventions based on mental skills training often used in practice, they focus on using them for simple, easily defined outcomes, such as enhanced motor-skill execution, increased physical activity, and self-confidence. New practitioners, however, find they have to use interventions for a larger variety of issues than those discussed in the literature (e.g. anger management). Beginning practitioners soon realize that the typical sport and exercise psychology interventions they have at their disposal (and the ones they were taught by lecturers and supervisors) need to be complemented by other interventions so they can help a wider range of people. One example is learning to use role plays to assist athletes to prepare for a meeting with a difficult or new coach; another might involve helping an exerciser with time management skills so they can schedule their workouts into a busy timetable.

Generally, most beginning sport and exercise psychologists acknowledge that they need to continue learning after their formal training has ended. The realization that lifelong learning is a feature of being a successful psychologist can stimulate exploration of new ways of working and helping athletes and exercisers. They may even enrol on seminars, workshops, courses, or qualifications to help them develop. As one example, in recent years mindfulness training has become a fashionable intervention to help clients. Sport and exercise psychologists who trained before mindfulness became popular are now attending workshops and reading textbooks to upskill themselves. As another example, sport and exercise psychologists may start reading the classic books on cognitive-behavioural therapy (CBT) if they were not exposed to them during training, delving into the works of the founding leaders, including Albert Ellis and Aaron Beck. It is understandable that the original CBT literature might be an initial port of call for some practitioners, because mental skills training is derived from CBT. Through reading the works of the original and influential CBT practitioners, sport and exercise psychologists gain an enhanced understanding of CBT, and this helps them understand clients' stories in new ways and expand the number of interventions in their toolbox.

One example where CBT might come into play involves golfers who experience anxiety and negative thoughts when putting. In many applied sport and exercise psychology textbooks, self-talk is discussed as a way to help people with anxiety, and the recommendation might be to make self-talk cues positive or motivational (e.g. "I can do this") to help athletes counter negative thoughts (e.g. "I can't do this"). Inexperienced sport and exercise psychologists may sometimes find that such recommendations do not help golfers (although often they do!), and the players may end up having "arguments" in their heads instead of playing their sports well. With further grounding in CBT, psychologists may start to help golfers examine the beliefs underlying their negative thoughts (e.g. some clients may think "I can't do this" because they believe they have failed to train properly and have a faulty swing). Having identified beliefs that may be leading to negative thoughts and anxiety, sport and exercise psychologists and golfers search for ways to test if those assumptions are correct. If the assumptions turn out to be false – perhaps after talking to their coaches golfers realize they are training properly and their swing is OK – then sport and exercise psychologists will help the golfers to change their beliefs. Psychologists might find that helping athletes confront and change their underlying beliefs allows them to reduce their negative thoughts and anxieties more effectively than trying to replace them with positive self-talk.

Another example where CBT might be useful involves adults who are not getting enough exercise for a healthy lifestyle and experience illnesses and conditions associated with weight management and poor cardiac health. Just telling people to go for a run or to do some exercise usually (almost always) does not help, but can make them feel even worse than they are already feeling. Using CBT ideas, however, sports and exercise psychologists can help people understand why they feel unable to exercise and find ways to improve their confidence and believe that they can make a positive change in their lives. Practitioners can also help people develop new coping skills that will ultimately improve their self-confidence: for example, improved time management skills will help them to achieve more, and this will build confidence. In recent years, employers in the NHS and other health and well-being industries have acknowledged that the knowledge and skills associated with sport and exercise psychology are necessary to help people improve their health and lifestyles, and they have created jobs that sport and exercise psychologists are well-qualified to fill.

A trainee's voice

It's certainly a challenging time, but you are certainly not alone in feeling like that. No matter how well you might have done in your education, nothing can quite prepare you for real life experience. But if you can see every experience as a learning opportunity then you will develop as an applied practitioner very quickly. When something happens, good or bad, try and think about it carefully and take something from it. These experiences are crucial to your development. They also give you some great stories to draw upon in interviews! In terms of knowledge base, don't feel like you need to answer athletes straight away. It's OK to allow yourself some time to think about the kinds of things you might suggest to them. It's easier to do this when you have a good relationship with the athletes and coaches, so your priority in any new environment is to build that relationship, which is often an effective intervention in itself!

Learning about boundaries and responsibility

Newly qualified sport and exercise psychologists are often excited to be working with clients and are intensely motivated to help clients improve performance and deal with their issues. Applied sport and exercise psychology often occurs at the venues where athletes and exercisers train and compete. Also, practitioners may go on tour with teams or attend training camps. Interactions with athletes may take place at any time of the day or night, on a bus, in a hotel lobby, at a cafe, by the side of a playing area, or in the car park. If you are at major tournaments like the Olympics, then you will find yourself working almost 24 hours a day! In comparison, other psychologists (including exercise psychologists) may work in traditional settings – such as in an office at a medical practice, counselling clinic, or leisure centre – and within well-defined time constraints (e.g. they may have 50-minute sessions with clients between the hours of nine and five). Sport and exercise psychologists who help both athletes and exercisers may spend some of their time at sporting events and some in their offices. The time and space boundaries in applied sport and exercise psychology can be looser and more ambiguous than in other sub-disciplines.

As a result of the looser boundaries and their strong desire to help people, inexperienced sport and exercise psychologists need to learn how to manage their time and interactions with some clients. To illustrate, one sport and exercise psychologist gave her mobile phone number to a client so that the person could contact her for assistance when they were not together. The client began to call the practitioner at all hours of the day and night, often waking the psychologist from sleep during the early hours of the morning. Often, the client was not experiencing a crisis but just wanted to chat. The practitioner realized that she needed to do something so she could get sufficient sleep. She started to operate two mobile phones: a work phone, whose number she gave to athletes, and a personal phone, whose number she gave to friends and family. She could then switch off her work phone while remaining in contact with loved ones if needed. Her voice message on the work phone gave details of how callers could get help if they were in crisis.

Learning how to apply ethical principles can be another learning experience for beginning practitioners. During training, sport and exercise psychologists learn about the BPS and HCPC ethical standards to which they need to adhere. If they have had good teachers and supervisors, then they may have been asked to reflect on their values and beliefs and been given opportunities to consider how they might behave when specific ethical situations arise. Once they are acting as autonomous practitioners, individuals begin to learn how integral ethical standards are to effective practice and success as a psychologist. Unethical practice may harm clients, hurt psychologists, and damage the standing of the profession. Unethical practitioners, for example, may quickly develop poor reputations. Poor reputations may discourage potential clients from approaching these sport and exercise psychologists, or they might find it difficult to secure employment.

Sometimes, however, it is not easy to uphold ethical standards in sport and exercise psychology because doing so may come at a cost. To illustrate, one practitioner we have talked to, who specialized in exercise psychology, was referred clients via a medical practice. One of the doctors was the boyfriend of the mother of a teenage client (who had been referred to the practitioner by the mother independently of the medical practice). The doctor wanted to find out about the teenager's progress. The practitioner would not disclose information because the doctor was not the teenager's legal guardian and the client had not given permission for the psychologist to share details with a third party. The doctor became aggressive and adamant he was entitled to the information. He also threatened to ensure the practitioner no longer got clients from the medical practice. The practitioner continued to withhold the information, but was worried about the potential loss of income. In this case, the doctor calmed down and apologized, and the practitioner still received referrals. Nonetheless, the story illustrates how ethical conflicts can arise in everyday practice, and how the emotional cost of maintaining the standards required of practitioners can be significant.

A trainee's voice

There are endless types of issues that new (and established!) practitioners face – some more head-scratching, jaw-dropping, and funnier than others! As a result, the profession's code of ethics is a guiding light for ALL parts of preparation, delivery and review – so understanding and upholding this code is essential. So is getting better at your professional judgement and decision-making. In short, if our job requires us to manage complex challenges and settings with excellent thinking, then we need to become and stay excellent thinkers! And as for the best thing about starting out, this all depends on the individual. Indeed, very rarely are things black and white in applied sport psychology – or any other people-focused profession for that matter. Be careful when this might seem to be the case because shades of grey (however many there are!) rule!

As newly registered sport and exercise psychologists resolve the challenges they encounter during the beginning years of their careers, they develop and grow as professionals, becoming better able to manage themselves and help their clients. One of the major changes observed in sport and exercise psychologists is a growing realization of how central a good relationship with clients is in service delivery. If there is not a relationship of respect and trust between clients and practitioners, it is difficult for psychologists to help clients. Related to this realization is the understanding that practitioners and athletes/exercisers collaborate, and each person is an expert in some way. Practitioners have expertise in psychology and clients have expertise in their own lives and sporting or exercise endeavours. Trainees often see themselves as expert problem-solvers who provide clients with special solutions to their problems. Through collaboration, however, sport and exercise psychologists assist clients to find their own solutions. Beginning practitioners realize they help clients to help themselves in resolving their own issues. Alongside this shift, sport and exercise psychologists realize they are not the superhero of the story, arriving to help clients with their problems and save the day. Instead, practitioners realize that clients themselves are the superheroes and sport and exercise psychologists play the role of the helpful sidekick. With experience, practitioners may also spend time reflecting on how their own tendencies, habits, motives, and histories influence the relationships they have with clients. Sport and exercise psychologists who regularly use their individual senses of humour in their work, for example, might need to carefully manage themselves when working with clients who have a different sense of humour from their own. As beginning practitioners develop their appreciation for the working relationship, they will often focus on developing their communication and counselling skills and may even attend additional courses and workshops.

A trainee's voice

I worked in all sorts of other jobs during my training and even immediately after qualification as I wasn't yet at the point where I was able to earn enough from just doing psychology. If you are the type of person who prefers to have one job and one salary, and it sounds unappealing (and stressful) to have to be self-employed and always hustle for work, you could consider an academic role where you are a lecturer and are able to practise sport psychology as part of that role – this is the route lots of people end up taking. That way there is a guaranteed salary each month, it's easier to do research and get published as well, and your consultancy can be developed via links your academic institution has with professional sport.

How you can help yourself learn after training and registration

You may have gathered from the preceding discussion that sport and exercise psychologists continue to learn a great deal about themselves and how to help clients after they have finished training. Effective practitioners learn and develop their skills and knowledge throughout their entire careers, partly because athletes, exercisers, the sporting/physical activity landscape, and society itself are constantly changing. For example, when we first began helping clients, the internet did not exist as it does today and mobile phones were not common. The lack of such media meant that we could not communicate with the athletes and exercisers we were helping as easily or as frequently as we can today. Learning to use the new media has stimulated changes in how sport and exercise psychologists can assist clients. It has also required practitioners to consider how ethical issues, and other issues such as marketing, confidentiality, and competence, apply to the use of new technology. Although these new technologies have enhanced the services that can be offered to clients, practitioners have had to learn how to use them in effective, safe, and ethical ways. We anticipate that technology will continue to evolve, and so practitioners will need to keep learning to stay up to date.

Sports, fashionable exercise programmes, athletes, and exercisers also change, providing another reason why sport and exercise psychologists have to keep learning. For example, the professionalization of rugby union is a major change that has occurred since we started our careers. Prior to 1996, rugby union was considered an amateur sport, and there were not the professional career pathways available to players that are present today. The possibility that rugby union players may now forge lucrative careers from the sport has added to the complexity of working with these athletes. As another example, in recent years high intensity interval training and other high-impact exercise programmes have become popular among exercisers wanting to fit a workout into their busy schedules. Such high-impact exercise can take a heavy toll on the body and may lead to people having injuries, especially if they did not learn correct exercise techniques. Having a major injury or even surgery can lead to some people experiencing negative emotions, and sport and exercise psychologists could help these people cope with their unhappiness.

Athletes' and exercisers' self-perceptions and associated behaviours have changed as well as the media and the environment. For example, scientists have found that over the last 40 years, the images of the ideal female and male bodies have changed in the media. The perceived ideal female body has become much more slender and athletic, whereas the ideal male body has become larger and a lot more muscular. During this same period, the levels of body dissatisfaction have increased in both men and women. Sport and exercise psychologists are among the people campaigning for warning labels to be placed on magazine adverts containing images of models, to let people know these pictures are often touched up/fake. Sport and exercise psychologists are also helping people improve their levels of body satisfaction to avoid consequences such as disordered eating and excessive exercise.

On a more positive note, exercise can improve people's body image and their self-perceptions. Sport and exercise psychologists can assist clients in starting exercise programmes that will best lead to positive self-perceptions.

Learn to reflect on yourself and your service delivery

Given the need to continually develop and adapt to changing environments and clients, it is useful to discuss how you can ensure that you grow and learn throughout your career. Reflection is the central mechanism by which sport and exercise psychologists develop their knowledge and skills for helping athletes and exercisers. Reflection involves thinking about your experiences, and asking questions such as what have I learned? What did I do well? What might I have done better? You might even reflect on future events and ask what is the best thing I can do to prepare? What might help me achieve my goals? There are lots of questions you can ask and sometimes it is good to talk about these questions with other people: reflection does not have to be a solitary exercise (Knowles, Gilbourne, Cropley, & Dugdill, 2014). A sport and exercise psychologist who has helped a runner prepare well for their first marathon, for example, may reflect and decide that part of his effectiveness was due to taking sufficient time to understand the exerciser's needs, whereas with previous clients he had been too quick to offer solutions. As an action to emerge from his reflection, he may decide that he will develop his approach to spend more time understanding clients' situations.

As another example, a sport and exercise psychologist feeling unsure about how helpful she will be to a rally driver with whom she has an appointment in a week's time may reflect and realize she had been worried because she did not have a good understanding of the sport. As an action to emerge from her reflection, she may decide to search the internet for information and videos and to seek out someone in her professional network who has experience of working in rally driving.

Learn from your clients!

When asked, practitioners often say that interaction with clients is the most common experience through which they reflect and learn about service delivery. To illustrate, one early career sport and exercise psychologist said that helping athletes was when "you have your opportunities to go out and test what you have learned, and learn from that direct contact with clients what works and what doesn't work" (Tod, Andersen, & Marchant, 2011, p. 105). Another practitioner said, "really one of the biggest lessons I took out of [working with athletes] was the need to know the athlete as a person before you try and work with the person" (Tod, Marchant, & Andersen, 2007, p. 324). When we consider that each athlete or exerciser is a unique person, living and playing sport or exercising within a distinctive context, we can appreciate why practitioners may say that every contact with a client is an opportunity to learn how to help people.

Learn from a supervisor

Supervision is another experience that allows sport and exercise psychologists to reflect on their skills and knowledge. Supervision for practitioners starting their careers involves a relationship with a more senior colleague who acts as a teacher, mentor, or guide. One newly qualified sport and exercise psychologist said, "Supervision gives you the insight into how to learn stuff from clients, because it gives you the necessary self-evaluation, and also evaluation of skills and questions and so forth, and self-reflection, that then allows you to actually learn something from the client, or allows you to learn more from the client" (Tod et al., 2011, p. 105). Historically, supervision has not happened as often as is desirable after individuals have qualified as sport and exercise psychologists, but the rules are continually changing in the UK and elsewhere, and it is possible that supervision will become mandatory for all practitioners throughout their careers (Tod & Lavallee, 2011), a change we will be delighted to see.

A trainee's voice

Once qualified, concerns [anxiety] might reappear. The competent, confident trainee becomes a "newbie" again, without the support of the structured training environment. I felt that I was allowed to make mistakes as a trainee but once qualified I felt the pressure of expectations on me to get it right all the time. I think that having a mentor or supervisor beyond qualification is essential and will make applied practice a far less pressurized experience.

Learn from being a client yourself

Another experience that helps practitioners grow is being a client themselves. From time to time, sport and exercise psychologists have difficulties and issues for which they may need some help, and they may visit a psychologist or counsellor. In addition to getting help with their issues, the opportunity to see another helping professional in action can help sport and exercise psychologists develop their skills and knowledge. One practitioner said she benefited from seeing a counsellor because it helped her understand "how a client might feel, because it is different, you sit in that chair [the athlete/exerciser's chair] and you feel really vulnerable; you sit in the practitioner's chair and you feel quite strong and confident" (Tod & Bond, 2010, p. 45). When asked about undergoing counselling, she also said:

> The counsellor I have, she's probably early thirties and she is self-employed. She has done something similar [to what I want to do] in that she has said "right I want to do this, I want to go into practice, and I'm going to become self-employed, I'm going to work in the private sector." Having someone that's been through that experience has been useful (Tod & Bond, 2010, p. 44).

Sport and exercise psychologists do not need to wait until they are having difficulties before seeing another psychologist or counsellor. Just as exercisers and athletes see a sport and exercise psychologist to find out how they might better achieve their sporting or exercising goals, practitioners can see a fellow helping professional to learn more about themselves and how they might get better at their jobs.

Learn from your personal life

Reflecting on your personal life can also help improve your skills and knowledge. A common example is your own sports or exercise participation. Most practitioners (admittedly not all) have played sport competitively or have engaged in exercise on a regular basis. Reflecting on their own participation might help practitioners understand what clients might think, feel, and do in certain situations, or might help them to develop new ways of using interventions. They might think about the people and events that led them to experience anxiety and how they coped with such negative emotions, thoughts, and physical sensations. Reflecting on non-sporting experiences may also be helpful. For example, sport and exercise psychologists may have achieved high levels of performance as actors, musicians, or dancers, and their attempts at mastering a publicly evaluated skill may provide them with insights into exercisers' or athletes' motives, desires, stressors, joys, and coping strategies. Equally, some psychologists have found that reflecting on unemployment, bereavement, injury, and other unpleasant experiences has helped them to empathize with clients who also encounter these events.

Learn from the literature

The scientific research and theory is another source of information on which sport and exercise psychologists can reflect and develop their knowledge and skills. If you decide to train and become a sport and exercise psychologist, you will hear lecturers, supervisors, and senior practitioners talk a lot about having a "theoretical orientation." A theoretical orientation is like a mental map in that it provides practitioners with explanations about the causes of distress and other issues athletes have, and suitable ways to help. For example, the CBT theoretical orientation includes discussion about how people's underlying beliefs interact with their feelings, behaviour, and environments to influence their state of mind. Knowing how these things interact allows sport and exercise psychologists to identify ways to help people change their beliefs. Once they start helping athletes, newly registered sport and exercise psychologists learn to appreciate the complexity of people's lives and how often a seemingly straightforward issue – such as anxiety, for example – can be influenced by many factors. For example, the list of factors that influence anxiety is long and any one or more of those items could be important for any specific exerciser or athlete. A theoretical orientation can help sport and exercise psychologists ask suitable questions to identity the relevant factors leading to clients' anxieties and the coping methods that may be helpful for that person.

There are many different theoretical orientations that sport and exercise psychologists can use, the most common one being the CBT approach (mentioned above). If you are interested, you could do an online search using the keywords *person-centred therapy, psychodynamic therapy*, and *humanistic therapy* to learn about some other approaches.

A trainee's voice

Finding a niche (once you are qualified) can be a good way to set yourself apart from others – many people focus almost exclusively on one sport, such as boxing and martial arts, or equestrian. I feel that my niche is developing more in the area of athlete well-being and addictions. However, although there are opportunities for independent practice and there are "some" jobs for sport psychologists, I think generally you should be prepared to have your fingers in several pies – many contracts for sport psychologists do not provide a full-time wage, and contracts can lose funding at any moment, the manager who hired you could get fired, and therefore you might not be around much longer than them, and people can be quite fickle when it comes to the benefits of sport psychology and how long they are prepared to wait to see results. So be prepared to always be looking for work, always looking ahead for when a contract ends, and perhaps also consider keeping other work or jobs for a while as your career develops.

Summary

In our opinion, one advantage of the UK pathway for sport and exercise psychologist training, as it is presently, is the amount of self-direction needed during the Stage 2 training process. Trainees are learning numerous transferable or extracurricular skills needed to survive and thrive as a sport and exercise psychologist in the UK – business acumen, networking and marketing skills, etc. These skills are sometimes not included in formal training programmes because they are squeezed out by other topics: there is just so much to learn! One result of learning transferable skills is that trainees may also realize that their competencies can be applied to a greater range of clients and contexts than helping just elite athletes in professional teams (with suitable upskilling of contextual knowledge). As we tell our students, over the course of your 40-year-plus career, many people are going to make a living and succeed as applied sport and exercise psychologists. There are few obstacles that you cannot overcome to be one of them if that is your dream.

Once you have realized your dream and become an HCPC-registered sport and exercise psychologist, the world is your oyster: yet what does that world offer from a career perspective? How should a career as a sport and exercise psychologist be conceptualized, and can you actually go on to make a career and a living for yourself? It takes a good chunk of time to train, so are the rewards and associated earning potential worth it? The final chapter looks at the present and future landscape of career possibilities for sport and exercise psychologists. Once again, the trainee voices are responding to the questions below:

Applying for jobs as a sport and exercise psychologist

What should you think about when applying?

What are employers looking for, and how do you make your application stand out?

What will an interview involve, and how should you prepare for it?

Career possibilities

Introduction

Most people beginning sport and exercise psychology undergraduate and master's degrees have a desire to become sport and exercise psychologists, and the focus of the current chapter is on career possibilities in the field. Some students, however, may not have envisaged themselves becoming sport and exercise psychologists, and other individuals may have a change of direction while they are completing their education. There are also some folks who decide to get a job at the end of their undergraduate studies to help pay for their postgraduate education or because they want a gap year. For these individuals, it is reassuring to know that the employment prospects of individuals with psychology degrees are robust when compared to other university qualifications and subjects. The vast majority of people graduating with psychology degrees are employed within six months of graduation. *Which?* magazine (2016) wrote that graduates of accredited psychology degrees had "a lower unemployment rate than average because its grads are so flexible and well-regarded by business. With a mix of good people skills and with excellent number and data handling skills, a psychology degree ticks most employers' boxes." The comments made by *Which?* were based on data from the Higher Education Statistics Agency, which can be found online (www.hesa.ac.uk).

Graduates of sport and exercise psychology undergraduate and master's degrees – like graduates of any psychology degree – have skills and attributes employers find valuable (such as self-discipline, the ability to work in and lead teams, the ability to network, and the ability to exercise independent critical thought) in addition to having knowledge about human behaviour. The BPS website (www.bps.org.uk) provides fantastic resources to assist psychology graduates. People with sport and exercise psychology undergraduate and master's degrees have much to offer and realize that success in the field is based on their ability to make a contribution to and meet the needs of others.

A trainee's voice

You need to be prepared to clearly detail the role and competencies of a sport and exercise psychologist as athletes and sporting organizations will have experienced many different practitioners with different approaches to service delivery and who have had different training. In many positions I have had to create my job description and present a proposal after a period in which I assess the needs of the client and/or sporting organization. You need to be creative and aware of the time it takes to prepare and feedback on sessions as the time that you actually spend with clients is just one part of your work. I think that the employers are looking for the sport psychologist to demonstrate a commitment to their goals and to clearly understand how in your role you can have an impact.

Individuals completing the postgraduate Stage 1 and Stage 2 training in sport and exercise psychology discussed in the previous chapters are embarking on a fantastically rewarding career, often in a domain about which they are passionate. During our careers, we have seen an increase in the types of jobs graduates obtain, and research focused on sport and exercise psychology reinforces our experience (Williams & Scherzer, 2003). Many of the jobs our graduates are finding and the ways they are now making a living were not in existence when we finished our education years ago, and given the pace of change in today's society, we believe current and future students will be able to create further opportunities for themselves and others in the future.

Becoming a successful sport and exercise psychologist is not easy. It takes effort, perseverance, creative thinking, and a commitment to serving clients' best interests. Education and work experience help students develop the necessary attributes and competencies so that they can realize their dreams and ambitions. We, and many of our colleagues, can attest that the effort and personal development often needed to succeed in the field are worth doing and add value, and the knowledge that you have helped athletes, coaches, exercise partici- pants, and others improve their lives and achieve their goals (and have been paid for doing so) is fulfilling. To help explore career possibilities in the field, the purpose of the current chapter is to (a) examine the various roles and specializations in the field, (b) discuss the possible employment settings, (c) explore possibilities in research and teach- ing, and (d) discuss possibilities in other countries. As with previous chapters, we will draw on the stories and advice of recent sport and exercise psychology trainees who are now themselves evidence of the career actualities we are about to describe.

The various specializations

For us, working as sport and exercise psychology professionals is hugely rewarding because the focus of our work is on helping people achieve their goals and dreams, create positive change for themselves, and enhance their well-being. Sport and exercise psychologists are helping professionals who enhance quality of life at the individual, group, and community levels. Before focusing on specific specializa- tions (sport, exercise, and performance), we will discuss ways in which sport and exercise psychologists contribute to positive change in people and communities.

Professionals in our domain are in the business of creating, com- municating, and applying sport and exercise psychology knowledge, and their roles involve researching, teaching, and consulting with ath- letes, coaches, and other stakeholders. As researchers, professionals create sport and exercise psychology knowledge that will help people increase their performance, improve their physical health, and live hap- pier lives. As one sporting-related example, researchers might explore how the words and images that people say to themselves or see in their minds (self-talk and imagery) can influence skill execution and athletic performance. Athletes might then use this information to help them say the words (e.g. "keep trying", "I can do it") to themselves or create the pictures in their minds (e.g. seeing themselves running fast) that will allow them to persevere when playing against tough opponents. From an exercise perspective, researchers might examine how making physical activity enjoyable might inspire people to spend more time exercising. Personal trainers might use such information to motivate clients.

A trainee's voice

I realized quite early on that I was going to need to diversify to (a) find work and (b) remain interested in the career I had chosen, as I was not especially motivated by the type of work that related directly to athlete performance, as some of my peers were. So during my training I specialized more in the exercise psychology side of the discipline, and because it is quite rare to meet someone who "just" wants to be more active, lots of my experience then and now has been with children, young people, and adults who wanted to lose weight – exercise and physical activity being just one of the lifestyle behaviours that needed to be tackled as part of being healthier, along with diet, alcohol intake, and smoking. So the more work I did in this area, the more I branched out from just exercise, into other areas of behaviour change.

A second role that sport and exercise psychologists perform is to translate research into useful information which they then communicate to others. As a prominent example, sport and exercise psychology professionals teach courses in universities and colleges as part of undergraduate courses, and postgraduate certificates and diplomas. Other examples include giving presentations, seminars, and workshops for professional sport and exercise-related organizations, such as being part of weekend coaching courses for specific sports. Professionals also write books, produce DVDs, or create websites as other ways to communicate sport and exercise psychology knowledge.

As a third role, practitioners also apply sport and exercise psychology knowledge directly with athletes, exercises, coaches, trainers, clients, teams, and other organizations. Sometimes in the media, elite athletes may talk about the benefits they have had from working with a specific sport and exercise psychologist. Although these media stories represent a common image of the sport and exercise psychologist, they do not sum up the only way professionals apply psychological knowledge. Professionals work one-on-one with many types of athletes, not just the elite. Sport and exercise psychologists may also work with groups, teams, and community organizations, depending on the clients' goals and resources. For example, instead of working directly with athletes, a psychologist might help a coach teach the athletes to use imagery or goal setting. Similarly, a psychologist may help a personal trainer to implement ways of assisting clients, or may help a non-profit organization to set up a community exercise programme for disadvantaged groups.

For many years, professionals have considered sport and exercise psychology to be a single field in which psychological principles are applied to the domains of competitive sport, physical activity, and exercise. As the field has developed, however, professionals have been able to specialize and research topics, offer academic courses, and work with clients focused on either sport or exercise. This reflects the sport psychology/exercise psychology discussion in the previous chapters, and having evolved towards different emphases in their own right, career possibilities now exist in both areas. Those focused on using sport psychology to address athletes' thoughts, feelings, and behaviours in competitive sporting contexts, may work at sports institutes or with professional teams. Individuals specializing in exercise psychology who focus on physical activity, exercise, and health domains, may work for councils, government departments, and health-related organizations. For psychologists in private practice or professionals working with sub-elite athletes, the differences in career focus are perhaps less explicit, because practitioners may need to help a variety of people across both settings for financial or other reasons.

In more recent years, many sport and exercise psychologists have started to demonstrate that they are not just interested or equipped to work in sport, but can offer services to performers from a variety of domains including the performing arts, business, and education. The skills that applied sport and exercise psychologists develop in the UK are applicable to many performance domains, and practitioners with suitable contextual knowledge know how to apply their skills to help a range of individuals. For example, a background in the performing arts may enable practitioners to assist musicians and actors with issues that parallel those from sport, such as learning ways to control performance anxiety, enhance skill learning, and prepare for performance exams. As you consider a career in sport and exercise psychology, you may also be able to identify other groups of people who may benefit from your knowledge and skills.

Employment settings

At a broad level, most sport and exercise psychology jobs fall into one of two domains: (a) research and teaching or (b) applied work. The distinction, however, is not absolute, and many professionals in the field engage in all three activities. There is some flexibility for professionals to tailor their work activity profile to best suit their desires and skill sets. Some of the sport and exercise psychology-related employment opportunities include being employed (a) by sports teams and bodies, such as institutes of sport, (b) in private practice, (c) by health, exercise, and medical-related organizations, (d) in education institutions, and (e) by corporate and professional development businesses.

Sports organizations

Individuals who complete Stage 1 and 2 postgraduate training find work in the sporting industry and with professional sports teams. In our experience, most students have working in professional and elite sport as a career dream. The phrase "it takes perseverance to be an overnight success" is useful advice we give these people. There are sport and exercise psychologists working in elite professional sport and we have seen the numbers expand over the course of our working lives. Many of these people, however, do not typically head straight into such employment settings full time right out of "school". These people may work at sub-elite levels for a period of time, building their professional networks and contacts and establishing a good reputation for themselves and the quality of their work. Given the pressures of the elite sporting environment and the focus on results, coaches, athletes, and sport administrators want to be confident that the people they hire will have something to offer and will make a good contribution to athlete performance and development.

Some organizations, however – such as the UK institutes of sport – may have internships and employment pathways that allow less experienced practitioners access to their environments. These types of internships may also exist overseas, most notably in the US. Although these internships may be competitive, they are worth exploring if you dream of working in elite sport. Mostly, they are highly sought after, and the organizations are able to select from a large number of candidates. Being aware of this competition now means that you can undertake activities during your training to make yourself more attractive, building networks, becoming familiar to the sporting high end environment, and if possible, engaging in relevant sport and exercise psychology activities (helping with research, shadowing experience practitioners, coaching, etc.).

We often come across students who are despondent because when they read the newspaper they do not see pages and pages of adverts asking for sport and exercise psychologists. We tell these people two things. First, over the course of their working lives there will be people who make a living in elite sport as sport and exercise psychology professionals, and there is nothing to prevent them from being one of those individuals if that is their dream and they are prepared to work hard towards achieving that goal. Second, although we are aware that sport and exercise psychology is a competitive industry, we point out that every profession these days is competitive. As an example, although there might be more jobs for lawyers or doctors than sport and exercise psychologists, there are also proportionately far more people wishing to enter those industries. It is a feature of today's society that valued jobs are competitive. That is not a reason to abandon your dreams and goals. Instead, it is useful information to help you think about how you can make yourself attractive to clients and employees.

A trainee's voice

Interviewers often present examples from their sport that they feel would benefit from psychology support and ask what you would do in such circumstances. You need to be able to clearly articulate your consulting philosophy and express how you can work both independently and within a multidisciplinary team. You need to get the balance between demonstrating expertise, knowledge and under-standing of your subject but not blinding athletes with science and theory. Make clear the evidence base to interventions but focus on demonstrating meaningful change as a result of your work. Finally, ensure that psychological development is separated from performance outcomes so that your work is not evaluated solely by whether a player or team wins or loses. If you are working on motivation make sure there is understanding of what progression looks like in this area.

Private practice and corporate and professional development businesses

A growing area for graduates is to become self-employed and start their own business. The expansion in self-employment in our field reflects a general trend of increasing self-employment in the UK. There is flexibility in self-employment and practitioners like the opportunity to be in charge of their working lives. One point to remember when considering self-employment is that you need to be clear on the services you are offering and to be strongly client focused. What service can you provide, and how is this different from what the team or organization has already? What can you provide that justifies them paying you? Another useful skill to have as a self-employed person running your own business is to know how to advertise yourself. For a person who is interested in being a consultant but is not yet ready to become their own boss, a possible starting point is to find employment in an existing consulting or professional development company. There are some successful professional development companies in the UK and making contact with these businesses as a student might help you start to develop networks.

A trainee's voice

If you are mostly interested in being an applied sport psychologist, then give some thought to whether you are comfortable being self-employed. A lot of the time, you create your own job by approaching teams or organizations that you think might be interested in what you have to offer, and then by doing a good job for them. Once you approach these

(continued)

(continued)

teams and organizations, some might pass on your information to their members for them to contact you directly; others might keep your information on file for when they feel they need a sport psychologist, and some might give you an opportunity to show them what you can do.

Rebecca Symes, whose "practitioner's voice" appears below, is an example of a sport and exercise psychologist who has assisted people in various fields, not just sport.

Rebecca's story

One career possibility available to people training in sport and exercise psychology is starting their own consulting business and becoming self-employed. Like any endeavour, self-employment has pros and cons. For example, many self-employed people have greater flexibility and independence over their working lives than individuals employed by an organization. Self-employed people may relish the opportunity to be their own boss and forge their own destinies; on the other hand, if they don't work then they don't get paid, unlike salaried employees. Also, many people who have moved from working for others to being self-employed have found that they work longer hours and may feel guilty if they take a holiday.

Rebecca Symes is a UK self-employed sport psychologist who has developed a growing business in the area. When Rebecca was a master's student, she started her own business, Sporting Success, and although this is not a rags to riches story, she is well on her way. Her story is illustrative for people considering sport psychology as a career, for several reasons. First, Rebecca has shown that opportunities exist for motivated individuals: if she can do it, then you can do it! Second, in writing about her story (Symes, 2014), Rebecca provides us with clues to her success. These clues are insights you could reflect on to help you decide if becoming your own boss is a desire you have.

Rebecca had a great desire to be her own boss. As she states, "There was something in me that really made me want to give it a go on my own, to see if I could make it. So I opened a business account, registered a website domain and set up an email address. Simple really. Now

I just needed some clients" (p. 107). As another insight, Rebecca has found work beyond the sporting context, including clients in schools and the corporate world. She has realized that the skills and knowledge she was taught as a sport psychologist are transferable to other domains, as we explained when we were talking about performance psychology. As a third insight, Rebecca is proactive in meeting people and promoting herself. If nobody knows you and what services you have to offer, then they are not going to ask you to help them. Along with meeting potential clients, Rebecca has built up a network of professionals, some of whom are other sport psychologists, and these contacts have also yielded clients. As part of their training, psychologists develop their communication and presentation skills so they are able to meet people and promote themselves. As Rebecca has said herself, "You have to be very proactive. Opportunities rarely drop on your doorstep and even if they do, you have to work very hard to ensure they come to fruition. I speak with a lot of students who contact me for advice and being proactive is one of the things I regularly say. I do believe there are opportunities out there for sport psychologists, but you have to be prepared to seek them out, build relationships, be patient, and to a certain extent make sacrifices in your own life. But, in my view, this is all worth it to be able to do a job that you love" (p. 111).

Possibilities in research and teaching

As discussed elsewhere, many sport and exercise psychology professionals are employed in universities to teach students and conduct research. Universities are not the only places, however, where sport and exercise psychology professionals teach or undertake research. Graduates of sport and exercise psychology degrees are employed in private research companies where the focus is on winning research contracts offered by a variety of funders including other corporate organizations, charities, and local and central government. Examples include helping to evaluate national walking programmes, understanding motivation and career transition for national and professional sporting bodies, and examining the mental health of athletes.

One difference between conducting research in a university setting and doing so in a private research company is that academics may have greater flexibility to pursue topics of their choice, whereas people in the private sector focus more on researching specific topics of special interest to the funder. As a result, academics may be able to develop lines of research that advance a body of knowledge about a particular area. On the other hand, researchers in the private setting may have greater variety in the topics which they have been asked to research. Each context may suit the different interests of people who want to be researchers: some individuals like variety whereas other folks like to focus on narrow areas.

Similarly, sport and exercise psychology graduates may also be employed to teach in further education institutions as well as in universities. Again, as with research, academics in universities may teach a narrower range of sport and exercise psychology topics than individuals in FE colleges. People in FE colleges may also have to teach sport-related topics such as sociology, health, or coaching as part of their portfolio. If you wish to teach students as part of your career it may be useful to ask yourself if you want to specialize, or do you like variety?

Although employed primarily to teach and conduct research, many academics also undertake applied work with athletes and thrive on doing all three activities. One advantage of engaging in all three activities is that research, teaching, and applied work then inform each other. For example, a sport and exercise psychologist who works with a team will likely be able to identify the research that will be most helpful to the sporting community. They will also be able to provide many real-world examples when teaching, and students will find their classes stimulating and educational.

As a final point to note in this section, having a PhD and being an academic provides individuals with skills and experiences that may allow them to secure employment beyond the UK boundaries, the focus of the next section.

A trainee's voice

Personally, I hope to combine lecturing with applied practice as I continue through my career, as not only do I enjoy both but I feel that they are inextricably linked. Evidence-based practice is essential and working in an academic environment tends to facilitate exposure to current research and the latest evidence.

Working in other countries

The UK belongs to a small select group of countries – such as Australia and Belgium – where sport and exercise psychology training and practice is regulated by professional statutory and regulatory bodies. In these countries, the titles "psychologist" and "sport and exercise psychologist," along with derivatives thereof, are protected by law. People advertising themselves as sport and exercise psychologists risk legal sanctions if they are not registered with suitable professional bodies, such as the HCPC in the UK. Across these countries psychological service delivery is also protected to varying degrees. Even if individuals do not market themselves as sport and exercise psychologists, they may risk sanctions if they have been deemed to be acting as one.

It is possible for UK trained and registered sport and exercise psychologists to obtain work in other countries where psychology training and titles are protected, provided that the country in which they wish to work recognizes their qualifications and experience. In these countries, there are normally professional bodies who will examine overseas (e.g. UK) qualifications and decide if they are equivalent to those approved and offered within that nation. For example, the Australian Psychological Society (APS) will assess UK academic qualifications in psychology for migration purposes. The APS assesses the level at which an applicant's qualifications are comparable to Australian-approved training to help people seeking to emigrate to Australia apply for registration, work as a psychologist in Australia, or apply for entry into an Australian-accredited psychology university course. Similar bodies and procedures exist in many countries where British citizens typically wish to work, including New Zealand, the US, South Africa, and Canada. The specific detail about what is needed in terms of qualifications and experience – along with titles individuals may use – varies with each country. To avoid unnecessary difficulties, it is worth learning about the exact requirements dictated by the country in question earlier rather than later (and these details may change as organizations review training and registration provision). The UK government keeps records of emigration and psychology is one of the popular emigration professions. Countries UK psychologists emigrate to include Commonwealth nations such as Australia, Canada, New Zealand, and Nordic countries such as Sweden, Norway, and Finland.

In many countries around the world, sport and exercise psychology training, service delivery, and titles are not regulated or protected by law. In some of these countries, there may be professional sport and exercise psychology, sport and exercise science, or psychology organizations that have *suggested* qualification and practice guidelines to help individuals plan their careers, but these are not legally enforceable. The degree to which these non-legally sanctioned guidelines are useful depends on the relationships the professional organization has with potential employers. For example, in the US, individuals may become "certified consultants" instead of a licensed psychologist. There is a good relationship between the US Association for Applied Sport Psychology (AASP) and the US Olympic Committee, and only AASP certified consultants may work with US Olympic athletes and teams.

In a few countries there may be avenues by which an individual can become a legally recognized practitioner psychologist, a sport and exercise psychology practitioner registered with another organization, or both. The US is one example, as mentioned above. New Zealand is another place where an individual can become a registered psychologist with the New Zealand Psychologist Board (a legally sanctioned title) or a mental skills trainer with Sport and Exercise Science New Zealand (a non-legally sanctioned title), or both. In both of the examples just given, there are procedures that allow UK citizens to have their qualifications assessed so that they can determine if they have met the requirements to be approved practitioners. Although we know people who have found employment in New Zealand and the US (along with other countries), we also need to say that the requirements for emigration and the transfer of qualifications change periodically as countries review their procedures and standards. Our best advice is that if you are interested in moving country, take the time to learn about the relevant qualifications and requirements and if possible tailor your training and professional development to allow you the best chance of realizing your ambitions.

The advice given above has been directed primarily towards people interested in working in other countries as practitioners and consultants. Currently, the situation is slightly different if you wish to work as a sport and exercise psychology academic overseas. University-employed academics in the UK and most other countries are typically selected based on their ability to teach and conduct research, with a PhD often being the minimum qualification needed. In this instance, you would need to show that you are capable of publishing research papers, winning research grants, teaching sport and exercise psychology courses, and supervising students doing research.

As a final piece of advice, if you are considering living and working overseas, then making contacts with individuals in the countries where you hope to obtain employment will help you to make the transition. These people will have relevant "insider" knowledge and may provide advice, direct you to suitable professional groups, let you know of upcoming jobs you can apply for, or even put you in touch with other people who may be useful contacts.

The following quote from a recent Stage 2 graduate provides insights into how to secure a job in sport and exercise psychology. This person was interested in being an academic, so the comments are relevant to obtaining a university position. At the end of the quote, the individual discusses getting applied work:

A trainee's voice

These days in academia a PhD is almost an essential requirement (even if the job ads say it is only a desirable one!). At application stage, follow the instructions carefully. If word counts are given, stay within them. In my view, the personal statement is probably the most important part of the application. HR departments can scan the other bits of the application to just tick off whether you meet the various criteria. After that has weeded several applicants out, a second sift will include reviewing candidates' personal statements to get a sense of who they are, their motivation for applying for the position, why they want this job, what they think they can bring to the role that sets them apart from others, and maybe a bit of their personality too. So spend time writing this. State clearly and methodically how you meet both the essential and the desirable requirements for candidates. Where you don't possess an essential or desirable quality, refer to it and show a solution for how you would address this limitation (for instance "I don't have experience of using the statistical analysis software STATA; however, I am very familiar with SPSS, and am

(continued)

(continued)

confident with learning new software"). Include your transferable skills that are not directly related to psychology or sport but make you a well-rounded candidate. If you are lucky enough to be shortlisted, interviews in academia are usually a panel interview, with a couple of faculty plus some human resources type people. You will probably be asked about your research interests and experience, and work experience lecturing, presenting, or teaching. You will be asked why you want this job, what your strengths are, and maybe your limitations. Interviews are often about "fit" and your personality as much as your education, skills, and experience. Have some questions planned for the end when you are inevitably asked whether you have any! "Can you talk me through a typical day/week?"; "Is there the opportunity to have training in. . .xxxx?" If there are research elements to the position (if it's a PhD studentship, for instance) you might be asked to talk about or present how you would approach the particular research study. Before you get to the interview stage, you might also be asked to develop a research proposal. If a job for an actual applied sport and exercise psychologist comes up – whether for a team, club, NGO etc. – you also need to take care with your application and your personal statement. If you get to interview you might be asked how you would approach a certain issue or problem from a psychological perspective, or to talk about your ideas for what you would do if you got the job. You would need to have done your research on the organization you are hoping to work with so that you can show that you have knowledge of the sport, and their context.

Summary

In this final chapter we have discussed career possibilities in sport and exercise psychology. Working as a sport and exercise psychology professional is rewarding and enjoyable, and is the key reason why we have both been employed in this area for most/all of our respective careers. If you like helping people improve the quality of their lives and work towards their dreams and you find exercise, sport, physical activity, and performance stimulating areas, then you may have a fulfilling career in sport and exercise psychology as well. We wanted to ensure that we included lots of practical advice and helpful ideas in this chapter to give you a realistic chance of securing employment. Jobs in sport and exercise psychology, as in all satisfying careers, are competitive, but you are at a stage where you can take steps to make yourself competitive and really stand out from the crowd when the time comes to look for work. Preparation makes a big difference. You can start your preparation today by developing the competencies and experiences needed to demonstrate that you can make a difference to an organization or client. As you gather information for job applications or marketing materials, put yourself in the shoes of the employer or athlete: what do they want and what are they prepared to pay you for? If it is a job, for example, try to find out as much as you can about the organization. The more you know about them, the easier it will be for you to show that you have the necessary skills, personality, and knowledge. Then when you are writing the application or promotion material, think about how you can present the information concisely and clearly. The easier you make life for the person reading your CV and support documentation, the less likely they are to discount you unfairly. Learning from our advice will help give you the most realistic chance of getting the job you want, whether it be working with elite sportspeople and other performers, helping fight the obesity epidemic in the UK, or teaching students so they can develop and pursue their hopes and dreams.

Finally, we hope you have enjoyed reading this book and have found it helpful in understanding how to become a sport and exercise psychologist. We also hope that you remain, or have become, more inspired to do so. We have enjoyed writing it and sharing our experiences of this fascinating and rewarding profession with you.

We wish you good luck wherever your career may take you!

References

British Psychological Society (2014a). *Standards for doctoral programmes in sport and exercise psychology.* Leicester: BPS.

British Psychological Society (2014b). *Standards for masters programmes in sport and exercise psychology.* Leicester: BPS.

British Psychological Society (2015). *Stage 2 qualifications in sport and exercise psychology candidate handbook.* Leicester: BPS.

Chandler, C., Eubank, M. R., Nesti, M., & Cable, T. (2014). Personal qualities of effective sport psychologists: A sports physician perspective. *Physical Culture and Sport. Studies and Research, 61,* 28-38.

Chandler, C., Eubank, M. R., Nesti, M., Tod, D., & Cable, T. (2016). Personal qualities of effective sport psychologists: Coping with organisational demands in high performance sport. *International Journal of Sport Psychology, 47(4),* 297-317.

Eubank, M. R. (2013). Professional training experiences on the qualification in sport and exercise psychology: A supervisor and candidate perspective. *Sport and Exercise Psychology Review, 9,* 45-60.

Eubank, M. R., & Hudson, J. (2013). The future of professional training for professional competence. *Sport and Exercise Psychology Review, 9,* 61-65.

Eubank, M. R., Nesti, M., & Cruickshank, A. (2014). Understanding high performance sport environments: Impact for the professional training and supervision of sport psychologists. *Sport and Exercise Psychology Review, 10,* 30-36.

Eubank, M. R., Niven, A., & Cain, A. (2009). Training routes to registration as a chartered sport and exercise psychologist. *Sport and Exercise Psychology Review, 5,* 47-50.

Fletcher, D., & Maher, J. (2014). Professional competence in sport psychology: Clarifying some misunderstandings and making future progress. *Journal of Sport Psychology in Action, 5,* 175-185.

Kanayama, G., Hudson, J. I., & Pope, H. G. (Jr) (2008). Long-term psychiatric and medical consequences of anabolic-androgenic steroid abuse: A looming public health concern? *Drug and Alcohol Dependence, 98,* 1-12.

Keegan, R. (2016). *Being a sport psychologist.* London, England: Routledge.

Knowles, Z., Gilbourne, D., Cropley, B., & Dugdill, L. (2014). Reflecting on reflection and journeys. In Z. Knowles, D. Gilbourne, B. Cropley & L. Dugdill (Eds.), *Reflective practice in the sport and exercise sciences: Contemporary issues*. Abingdon, England: Routledge.

McEwan, H. E., & Tod, D. (2015). Learning experiences contributing to service delivery competence in applied psychologists: Lessons for sport psychologists. *Journal of Applied Sport Psychology, 27*, 79-93.

Nesti, M., & Littlewood, M. (2011). Making your way in the game: Boundary situations in England's professional football world. In D. Gilbourne & M. B. Andersen (Eds.), *Critical essays in applied sport psychology* (233-250). Champaign, IL: Human Kinetics.

Symes, R., (2014). Sporting success. In P. McCarthy & M. Jones (Eds.), *Becoming a sport psychologist* (105-111). London, England: Routledge.

Tod, D., & Andersen, M. B. (2005). Success in sport psych: Effective sport psychologists. In S. Murphy (Ed.), *The sport psych handbook* (303-312). Champaign, IL: Human Kinetics.

Tod, D., & Andersen, M. B. (2012). Practitioner-client relationships in applied sport psychology. In S. Hanton & S. D. Mellalieu (Eds.), *Professional practice in sport psychology: A review* (273-306). London, England: Routledge.

Tod, D., Andersen, M. B., & Marchant, D. B. (2011). Six years up: Applied sport psychologists surviving (and thriving) after graduation. *Journal of Applied Sport Psychology, 23*, 93-109.

Tod, D., & Bond, K. (2010). A longitudinal examination of a British neophyte sport psychologist's development. *The Sport Psychologist, 24*, 35-51.

Tod, D., Eubank, M. R., & Andersen, M. (2014). International perspectives: Training and supervision in the United Kingdom and Australia. In J. G. Cremades & L. S. Tashman (Eds.), *Becoming a sport, exercise, and performance psychology professional: A global perspective* (324-330). New York: Psychology Press.

Tod, D., & Lavallee, D. (2011). Taming the wild west: Training and supervision in applied sport psychology. In D. Gilbourne & M. B. Andersen (Eds.), *Critical essays in applied sport psychology* (193-215). Champaign, IL: Human Kinetics.

Tod, D., Marchant, D., & Andersen, M. B. (2007). Learning experiences contributing to service-delivery competence. *The Sport Psychologist, 21*, 317-334.

Which? (2016). *Psychology courses*. Retrieved from http://university.which.co.uk/subjects/psychology

Williams, J. M., & Scherzer, C. B. (2003). Tracking the training and careers of graduates of advanced degree programs in sport psychology, 1994 to 1999. *Journal of Applied Sport Psychology, 15*, 335-353.

Index